LIVING
PROOF

LIVING
PROOF

Onyx Moonshine's Journey

TO REVIVE THE AMERICAN SPIRIT

 BUSINESS PRINCIPLES FROM
THE MIND OF A MOONSHINER

ADAM VON GOOTKIN

CAREER
PRESS

THE CAREER PRESS, INC.
WAYNE, NJ

Copyright © 2016 by Adam von Gootkin

All rights reserved under the Pan-American and
International Copyright Conventions. This book may not
be reproduced, in whole or in part, in any form or by any
means electronic or mechanical, including photocopying,
recording, or by any information storage and retrieval sys-
tem now known or hereafter invented, without written
permission from the publisher, The Career Press.

LIVING PROOF
EDITED BY LAUREN MANOY
TYPESET BY KRISTIN GOBLE
Cover design by Faceout Studio
Cover photo of bottle by Nick Caito
Printed in the U.S.A.

To order this title, please call toll-free 1-800-CAREER-1
(NJ and Canada: 201-848-0310) to order using VISA or
MasterCard, or for further information on books from
Career Press.

The Career Press, Inc.
12 Parish Drive
Wayne, NJ 07470
www.careerpress.com

Library of Congress Cataloging-in-Publication Data

CIP Data Available Upon Request.

Dedication

To the American Spirit.

ACKNOWLEDGMENTS

The process of launching Onyx Spirits Company and of writing this book to share that tale has been a lot of hard work. Without the Onyx team and my family, there would be no story to tell.

I would like to thank first and foremost Pete, the constant yin to my insane yang; whose statement "Let's make moonshine" changed the course of our lives for eternity. I thank Jacque, who listened to me rant and rave for more than a year, through the writing of this book. A special thanks to my agent, Bob Diforio, whose open mind allowed this book to be. A thanks to Quin, who named this book *Living Proof.* And I thank Rachael, who chose the cocktails at the end of each chapter.

There have been many people who have helped us professionally to get to this point, whom I would like to thank: Ken Yandow, Mike Donovan, Dave Heller, Andy Quinn, Victor Lugo, Geoff

Luxenberg, Bob Mule, Mike Polo, Tom Kowalczyk, and Anthony Viscogliosi.

Last, I thank my family, to whom I dedicate my work. To my wife Regina, whose belief and love has never waivered. To my mother, who made me want to write. I thank my uncle Bob and uncle Brian, who taught me to both dream and execute. And to my grandmother, fairy godmother aunts, brother, and cousins.

If I've left anyone out, it's not because you're not important. I've had a lot of moonshine tonight.

Cheers, friends. As we journey through life, let us live by the way.

CONTENTS

PROLOGUE / 11

FOREWORD / 15

CHAPTER 1 / 21
McDonald's, the Military, or College:
Why Taking the Road Less Traveled Really
Does Make All the Difference

CHAPTER 2 / 51
Overwhelm Your Obstacles With Passion: Believing
in Your Dream When No One Else Will

CHAPTER 3 / 77
Find Your Peter: Surrounding Yourself With People Who
Support Your Strengths (and Make Up for Your Weaknesses)

CHAPTER 4 / 97
Chase the Insatiable Horizon: The Art of
Setting—and Reaching—Your Goals

CHAPTER 5 / 117
Trillions of Dollars in the Air: Tapping Into
the Abundance All Around You

CHAPTER 6 / 143
Rock Bottom to Bottoms Up: Why Falling
Behind Is Key to Moving Forward

CHAPTER 7 / 161
Anything They Can Do, You Can Do Better:
Turning Mediocre Markets Into Goldmines

CHAPTER 8 / 183
Snooze You Lose, Booze You Win: Seizing
Opportunity Before It's Too Late

CHAPTER 9 / 203
The Entreprenuer's Dilemma: Weighing the
Pros and Cons of Micromanaging a "Small
Business" Versus Big-Picture Thinking

CHAPTER 10 / 221
Socially Conscious Commerce: How Your Business
Can Make the World a Better Place

INDEX / 235

ABOUT THE AUTHOR / 239

PROLOGUE

I have a deep-seated, possibly genetic, love for moonshine and whiskey. I also love the creation of business only slightly more than making money and the freedom it buys. So I threw it all together, fermented it, and distilled out this book.

Writing this book allows me to address a constant itch I have to inspire would-be entreprenuers to take a leap of faith. In my experience, entreprenuers embrace helping other entreprenuers, as we are all part of some not-so-secret struggle club that no one on the outside can ever truly understand.

Our tale is one of family legacy, innovation, and loads of hard work driven by passion. If this book causes even one of you to clock out of the cubicle for the last time and pursue your dream, I'll consider it a win.

Not that I'm some globally successful billionaire entreprenuer (yet). When I looked at buying Friendly's founder, Prestley Blake's, recreation of

Thomas Jefferson's mansion, Monticello, Mr. Blake higlighted the helicopter landing area. I replied that my helicopter was "in the shop." By helicopter, I was referring to the RC helicopter I'm fond of flying around my office into unsuspecting people's hair.

At 32 years old, I have been an entreprenuer my entire life. My last real "job" was working as a pool cabana boy until I was 18. That was pretty sweet, as I was surrounded by bathing suit–clad females, giving me the time to read Dale Carnegie's *How to Win Friends and Influence People* as well as every book by Brian Tracy over and over again. Hot chicks and business adventures—yeah, pretty much the afterlife. Sometimes I wish I just kept that job, but destiny beckons.

Failing out of college and living as an entreprenuer has given me a unique perspective because I'm always on the outside looking in. I see friends and colleagues who are consistently making money for other people, ignoring their calling, and chasing the money train to the grave. I'd rather be farming or collecting bottles for the 5-cent return. As far as I'm concerned, anything beyond that independent simplicity is a luxury. Maintaining that mindset creates a delusional happiness—bordering on insanity—that ensures you're always winning in your mind, which will manifest itself to reality.

In the incredibly vibrant world we live in today, always shrinking with technology growing at an exponential rate, I believe opportunity is more abundant than ever in human history. Access to people, funds, ideas, and resources is networked directly to the smart phone in your pocket. If you're not waking up with a smile every day, excited to face the world, make a change, damn it!

When my family was arrested for evading the tax on their whiskey in 1864, we lost our distillery. I highly doubt they could have foreseen our revival 151 years later, never mind a book about it. Now *that's* the American spirit. Here's to persistence!

So pour yourself a glass of Onyx Moonshine or our Secret Stash Whiskey (or double-fist that ish for a game of Edward 40 Hands), and let's talk about success.

Cheers!

Adam von Gootkin

Co-Founder

Onyx Spirits Co., LLC

FOREWORD

The American Spirit is born out of our country's legacy of being the land of opportunity. We all have the privilege of living in the land of the free, not the land of entitlement. You and I have the same opportunity to do or be absolutely anything we want in this life. I don't care what your background is, whether you had a tough upbringing, are an immigrant, or have faced any other struggles. Because we live in America, you have the opportunity to grow and do something special and achieve greatness. In America, the opportunities are endless. Some people are not willing to work for it, and that's one of the biggest problems I see in our country right now. When you have an entrepreneurial spirit like Adam von Gootkin, who founded a company like Onyx Spirits, which has created a great product and a great following from nothing, it truly embodies the American Spirit. Onyx was created on their own initiative; two entrepreneurs saw an opportunity and they've worked hard to take advantage of it. Anyone can do it if they're willing to focus and put in the work.

We live in an age where there is too much entitlement. I believe in helping people, but I believe more in helping people to help themselves. I want to put people in a position where they can succeed by working, by having initiative, by focusing their drive and getting results. I think that's the most important thing and that is the definition of the American Spirit.

To be successful in life, in business, in football, in moonshine, you've got to have a goal. Ask yourself: What's your goal? You may say, I wanna do this, or I wanna do that, and that's fine. But how are you going to reach that goal? Do you have methods, do you have a technique, are you making small changes to your life every day? You need to make the decision to succeed. You need to work at it. You need to be obsessed with it. You need to give it your all. You want to be a great football or baseball player? Great, the only way to get there is through practice. Now, it may or may not happen, but one thing is absolutely certain, it will *never* happen if you don't set the goal, work at it, practice, and discipline yourself to do the right things. The people who win Super Bowls are the ones who are out there putting the time in, the effort in; they put the sweat in. And that's what the American Spirit is all about: hard work.

People sometimes think that because they're not rich, that they don't have any opportunity. I defy anybody who tells me that's why they can't succeed. If you're willing to work at it, I don't care what your financial status, nationality, or religion is: You can do absolutely anything you want to do. You just have to want it. Sometimes I think the American Spirit is dying, but I believe the core is still there. Our grandkids may not know or understand much of what we've gone through because times are changing. There will always be those who will succeed and prosper, and there will always be those who walk around with their hand out waiting for someone to save them. The ones who succeed and prosper through hard work and focus are the ones who will bring our country to the next level.

Ultimately, I think the entrepreneurial spirit is of the utmost importance. It makes our country great. It's essential for the future. I've heard people say that "everything's been invented already," but it hasn't. There is opportunity everywhere. Think about a problem and find the solution. Every day scientists and innovators are making major improvements to every type of technology we have. Think back to the 1940s, to the early cars and the first color TV. People asked, "How it could get better than this?" Now we have cars driving themselves and TVs in the palm of our hands! Everything in our society is there because people have created it. People are improving on products every day, and anyone can do it if you put your mind to it.

Primarily, my goals in life have been to be a great coach, to reach the playoffs, and to win the Super Bowl with the Bears. I was hands on and I believed in my goals, myself and my team. My cigar line, my wines, my restaurants, and my other entrepreneurial projects are there because I've partnered with great people who know how to do what they do. Putting smart people in the right places is one of the most important things you can do to succeed in life and achieve your goals. Having a great team is an integral part to success. When your team wins, you win.

In my mind, the greatest thing I've created was an attitude with the Bears. The attitude was that we were going to win the championship, and we did. We were willing to sacrifice and willing to work hard. I had a group of good guys around me who were willing to pay the price, and we had a lot of great leadership. Working together as a team propelled us toward victory, and we couldn't have done it if everyone wasn't committed to the goal.

At the end of the day, you have three options: Lead, follow, or get the hell out of the way.

Coach Mike Ditka

CHAPTER 1

MCDONALD'S, THE MILITARY, OR COLLEGE

Why Taking the Road Less Traveled Really Does Make All the Difference

It all started with a mouse. Or perhaps I should say, it all started with a horde of mice. A horde of tiny, hairless, squirming pink mice that magically appeared in their mother's cage overnight during the summer of 1993. I stared into the now-crowded quarters of my 6-year-old brother Josh's pet rodent, Gizmo, with equal parts fascination and disgust. As the older sibling—I was 10 years old at the time—I couldn't help but feel the sudden weight of responsibility bearing down on my young shoulders. Those creepy little creatures would get big fast.

"What are we going to do with 20 mice?" I wondered aloud. "There's no way we can keep them all."

"We should sell them," said Josh.

I didn't know it at the time, but those words would change my life.

Our mother, perhaps unsurprisingly, agreed that selling Gizmo's offspring to the local pet store was a fine idea. And so off we went to convince the owner of our local pet store in Rocky Hill, Connecticut, that two sticky-faced, grubby-fisted kids with a boxful of baby mice should be his new snake food suppliers. It was my first business deal. Over the course of that summer, our impressively fertile mama mouse gave birth to several more litters of babies, resulting in a total revenue of about $200 for Josh and me. Sure, it might not sound like much now, but we were kids and money was tight. At the time I was fairly certain we could retire for life. Our parents had divorced two years prior, and my mother supported us by working long hours running a local daycare center. Thanks to her tireless efforts, and those of the rest of my family, my brother and I always had everything we needed. I didn't need the treats and toys I bought with the money we made from selling mice. But I sure as hell wanted them.

That first taste of success stuck with me. I gave people (or, in this case, snakes) what they wanted and got what I wanted in return. Seemed like a pretty good deal. Still, my next foray into the free market two years later was purely accidental. It was time for Corpus Christi Middle School's annual candy fundraiser. Like the rest of the students, I was given a box filled with Caramello bars to peddle door to door for a buck each, preying on unsuspecting neighbors in need of a sugar fix. There was only one problem with this arrangement: I discovered a passionate love for Caramello bars. Surely no one would notice if I took one or two for myself, right? Possibly three? If an even number were missing, maybe it would be less noticeable, I reasoned. Better to eat four.

I'm sure you can see where this is going. Over the span of two short days, I gobbled up the contents of that cardboard box like Augustus Gloop from Willy Wonka's chocolate factory. Before I could stop myself, those 30 Caramello bars were gone, their shiny brown wrappers stuffed into the bottom of my trash can (as if obscuring the evidence would somehow clear me of wrongdoing). I started to panic. Now I owed my school $30! I didn't have that kind of money, and I certainly couldn't ask my mother for the cash. Then, sort of like the Grinch Who Stole Christmas, I got an idea. An awful idea. I got a wonderful, awful idea: What if I told my teacher that I sold the whole box of candy and needed another, then sold those Caramello bars for twice the price?

My plan went off without a hitch. As it turned out, most people felt that $2 was a perfectly fair price for a Caramello bar. I'd figured out a way to pay my school the cash I owed and feed my Caramello habit: the proverbial win-win. Sweet.

Thanks to Catholic schools' well-known affinity for snack-based sales, candy would feature prominently in the next phase of my entrepreneurial development as well. Football was a major focus at Xavier High School in Middletown, Connecticut, and there were many sales devoted to benefiting the team. I couldn't afford to play sports (participating would have tacked another $1,000 or so on to the tuition my mother and other extended family members were already struggling to pay), but that didn't stop me from participating in fundraising efforts—in my own way. I'll never forget the moment inspiration struck. It was around 11:00 a.m. on a Tuesday. Running late, I rushed into my second-period math class to find that none of my fellow classmates were at their seats yet; instead, everybody was gathered around one desk in the center of the room. Sitting at the desk was Big George, Xavier's star linebacker. In the center of the desk was a cardboard box filled with candy bars—M&M's, Skittles, even my beloved Caramello bars. I moved closer to the edge of the throng and watched as kids threw—literally threw—money at the football player. Victims of mid-morning blood sugar crash, I guessed. George had picked a genius time of day to whip out that box of candy. Not only was he giving people what they wanted, he was giving it to them when they wanted it most. The only flaw in George's system, as far as I was concerned, was that all of his profits were going to the team, a mistake I would be sure to avoid.

Before I go any further, allow me to explain: When I said money was "tight" while I was growing up, I meant that more often than not, I didn't even have enough pocket change to buy lunch. So when I figured out a way to cash in big on my school's fundraiser, I didn't feel terribly guilty. I needed the money, or I wouldn't eat. Besides, my "crime" would be victimless—sort of.

After class that day, I approached George's desk. "All out of candy, dude," he said, thumbing through a stack of dollar bills. "That's cool," I said, trying to sound casual. "Hey, are you done with that cardboard box? Do you still need it?"

George looked up from his wad of cash. "Nah, I was just gonna throw it out," he said, shrugging. "You can have it, if you want."

"Thanks," I said, in the most nonchalant manner possible, and picked up the box. Score.

My next move was to call my Aunt Kathie, who had a membership to Sam's Club. Candy bars sold in bulk at Sam's Club for 30 cents each. If Kathie would take me to Sam's and let me use her membership, I figured I could fill up that empty cardboard box and sell them at school for a dollar apiece, like George. Everyone would just assume the money was going to the football team.

As with the Great Caramello Bar Caper, my plan went perfectly—better than perfectly, in fact: The candy sold out in less than an hour, 30 bars multiplied by a profit of 70 cents each came out to $21, which was a lot more than I would have made in an hour mowing lawns or washing dishes in a diner. I started collecting George's empty cardboard boxes and told my aunt I would need another ride to Sam's Club in the near future. Before long, my sugar shakedown was getting almost too successful for me to handle on my own. It was time to expand my operation. I rounded up a couple of kids from each grade who were enterprising and trustworthy (but not so trustworthy that they'd be opposed to some good old-fashioned business) and explained that if they would be willing to help me out with sales, I'd split the profits. We met each morning at my car. They would hand over the money they earned the day before, and I would give them their share of the cash, fill up their boxes, and send them off in search of kids who forgot to eat breakfast. I was like Xavier's own Willy Wonka. My locker had literally become a candy supply closet; the trunk of my 1987 Volvo was packed full of crates of corn syrup–laden junk food. Within a few months, my "staff" and I had pulled in thousands of dollars. I had never, ever seen money like that, and it was beyond thrilling. At a certain point, however, so many kids started asking me for boxes that I began to get concerned. My school was very strict and it was only a matter of time before one of the administrators figured out what was going on; in fact, I'd heard whisperings of an investigation. So I pulled the plug on our candy con. Years later, I made an anonymous donation to my school to assuage a bit of the lingering guilt I felt. In the process, I found out it felt pretty good to give back.

It was sad to see the inevitable fall of my empire, but I really couldn't complain. We'd had a good run, after all. Really good. Look, I won't pretend that all my earnings were spent on sensible things like lunch. I loved, and still love, to entertain and share my success with friends and family. And some of it was spent on showing off—by which I mean buying endless rounds of cocktails for my friends at a local bar. The fact that we were underage didn't present as much of a problem as you might think, thanks to the trusty suit my aunts had bought me for school several years earlier. Somehow, it didn't matter that I had the face of a choirboy; when I bellied up to the bar dressed to the nines with a big smile, chatting about my long day, the bartender didn't think to ask for an ID. Neither did the next bartender, or the next. Why would they, when the first bartender recommended me? They didn't question the legal status of my "work associates," either. Playing Mr. Big with my buddies at the bar at the age of 16 was a blast, I'm not going to lie. But the experience also played a crucial role in my professional growth. Henry Ford said, "Whether you think you can, or think you can't, you're right." I had no experience in the business world, but imagining for an evening that I was a hotshot career person made me feel like I'd already hit the big time. Convincing a bunch of bartenders that I was a responsible adult with a job so demanding I required a stiff drink by the end of the day made me realize that people rarely question confidence. Even if you have no idea what you're doing.

That's not the only knowledge I gained from my stint as a high school candy hustler. Looking back, I can see how the experience served as my first introduction to several fundamental business principles:

- Give the market what it wants, when it wants it.
- Delegation is essential to amplifying your purpose.

- To manage people, you have to inspire them and treat them well.
- Reinvesting profits is key to business growth.
- Making your business legal and legitimate means it's less likely to evaporate into thin air.

So I guess you could say I learned quite a bit in high school, even if I didn't learn it through conventional methods like pop quizzes and study breaks. But then, traditional education was never a great fit for me. I was a *D* student at best, even failing Spanish, a language I've been fluent in since childhood. For as long as I could remember, I found school to be exceptionally boring. I always felt like I was being programmed to live a mediocre version of somebody else's life rather than to figure out the best way to live my own. Authority for the sake of authority made absolutely no sense to me. I was hardwired to question everything and suspected anyone who demanded my respect without earning it first of not deserving respect at all. Consequently, I had less than no motivation to do what other people told me to do, particularly if I didn't fully understand why

I was supposed to do something. It wasn't that I was opposed to learning. I was a voracious reader with an unquenchable curiosity about life in general. Even though we didn't have much money, my mother's rule was that she'd always buy us any book we wanted. Books were my best friends as a kid—any books I wasn't being forced to read, anyway. Years later, I would read a quote by Albert Einstein that summed up my exact feelings as a student:

> School failed me, and I failed the school. It bored me. The teachers behaved like Feldwebel (sergeants). I wanted to learn what I wanted to know, but they wanted me to learn for the exam. What I hated most was the competitive system there, and especially sports. Because of this, I wasn't worth anything, and several times they suggested I leave. This was a Catholic School in Munich. I felt that my thirst for knowledge was being strangled by my teachers; grades were their only measurement. How can a teacher understand youth with such a system? From the age of 12 I began to suspect authority and distrust teachers.

I learned mostly at home, first from my uncle and then from a student who came to eat with us once a week. He would give me books on physics and astronomy. The more I read, the more puzzled I was by the order of the universe and the disorder of the human mind, by the scientists who didn't agree on the how, the when, or the why of creation. Then one day this student brought me Kant's *Critique of Pure Reason*. Reading Kant, I began to suspect everything I was taught. I no longer believed in the known God of the Bible, but rather in the mysterious God expressed in nature. (*ToerMagazine.com/2014/05/03/641*)

A distrust of formal education wasn't the only thing I shared with Einstein. My uncle—in fact, both of my uncles—taught me more about the world and my place in it than any teacher. My Uncle Bob, who was married to my mother's sister Charlene, was and is my ultimate inspiration. An African-American man, he grew up in the South when segregation was still in full swing, forced to drink at separate water fountains and use different restrooms. His grandparents were slaves. But

Uncle Bob didn't let any of that stop him from reaching his impressively lofty goals. Now a global executive at Dell, Uncle Bob taught me the importance of not just working hard, but working smart; of incorporating wisdom into all you do, and of doing it with charm and charisma. Essentially, he taught me all the fundamentals of Dale Carnegie's *How to Win Friends and Influence People* years before I discovered the book. He also taught me that we all have the same opportunities in life, no matter how humble our beginnings. Once I asked him if he ever felt intimidated when he had to give presentations in front of large, important crowds— or even in a meeting with billionaire Michael Dell. "Everybody puts their pants on one leg at a time, Adam," he told me.

My Uncle Brian, a gifted restorer of classic American muscle cars, was a self-made man of a different stripe. My first "real" business experience would come from helping him launch his muscle car restoration business shortly after I graduated high school. Detail-oriented to a fault, Uncle Brian drilled the following credo into my head: Nothing is worth doing unless you intend on doing it better than anyone else.

I was lucky to have such galvanizing, admirable adults in my family, especially because, as I mentioned, there wasn't much inspiration to be found in the authority figures at school. This was never more apparent than during my senior year when I sat down with my guidance counselor to talk about my future.

"Basically, you have three options," he said from across his desk. "You can work at McDonald's, join the military, or go to college."

"That's it, huh?" I asked.

"That's it," he confirmed.

I should mention that although I had my problems with Xavier, and Xavier with me, I think I got the most out of it I could and look back at my years there fondly. Being a college prep school, their job was to get me into college. Still, not every kid is meant to formally extend his or her education past high school. That's why now, many years later, I'm working to propose an entrepreneurship program for schools in the hopes that going forward, students will have a fourth option to choose from. Anyway, back then in my counselor's office, I wasn't thrilled about any of the options offered to me but because all my friends were going to college, I figured I might as well, too. Somehow, in spite of my less-than-stellar grades, I managed to get into Roger Williams University as a double major in international business and languages. It was a big deal. I was the first person in my family to go to a university, and my aunts and Uncle Bob were so thrilled that they agreed to help pay my tuition. I did my part by taking out some smaller loans. Actually, thrilled might not be the best word to describe my uncle's reaction; in fact, I vividly remember Uncle Bob having the foresight to say that he was only helping me because of my Aunt Charlene. He did not believe college was for me. Unfortunately, when I got to Roger Williams, I realized pretty quickly that he was right. College, it seemed, wasn't going to be all that different from high school. My first disappointment was upon finding out that none of the professors teaching my entrepreneurial courses had ever run businesses themselves. What could these people possibly have to tell me about getting ahead in the real world? Granted, there were some useful experiences to be had at university. For example, I became the youngest person ever elected to student senate. (I also set up an extremely successful "import" business, but

I'll save that story for another book.) In that sense, those tuition dollars weren't entirely wasted. But the fact that I saw no point in going to my classes was a huge problem as far as administration was concerned. When I went home for winter break, there was a letter waiting for me: I would not be welcome back at school when the new semester started. That was it. The party only lasted 16 weeks.

Even though I was ever so slightly relieved, the prospect of having to break the news to my family weighed heavily on me during the holiday. I was supposed to be our clan's inaugural college graduate, and I had flunked out after just one semester. Worst of all, my relatives thought I'd been doing well at school.

I made up my mind to tell everyone the truth when we were all together for Christmas at my aunt and uncle's place in Watch Hill, Rhode Island. It was probably the single most uncomfortable conversation of my life. My mother, aunts, and uncles didn't bother to hide their frustration, and I couldn't blame them. They'd made sacrifices for me, and I let them down. I felt absolutely horrible.

Later that day, I took a long walk down the beach. I walked until I couldn't walk anymore, and then I sat down on a rock at the water's edge. The damp winter wind whipped against my face as I watched the cold gray waves crash into the sand. What the hell was I doing with my life? At that point, I honestly didn't know—but deep down inside, I did know that college wasn't the place for me. Still, where did I belong? In that moment, my guidance counselor's words came back to haunt me: McDonald's, the military, or college. Out of my two remaining options, is it any wonder I chose the military?

It was 2002, and America was invading Iraq. Being patriotic by nature, my mother drove me from her house, where I'd moved back to, into the Navy recruitment office, making me promise not to sign up right away. I took a test. Ironically (given the fact that I'd just flunked out of college), I must have done rather well on that test because they offered me an E-3 intelligence position right away. I was going to be sent to school to learn intelligence and languages (Arabic and Chinese); eventually I would be placed on a submarine. The submarine part did sound pretty cool, I have to admit. Almost before I knew what was happening, I signed up to ship out in two months. Sorry, Mom.

Around this time, I'd been getting to know my now-business partner, Peter Kowalczyk. He was three years older than me and a hospitality major at the University of Massachusetts in Amherst. We'd met at a party at his house and hit it off right away. One night, we were sitting around his house drinking cognac and talking, and we realized that we both loved to read. Pete ran up to his bedroom and returned with a stack of books a mile high. We talked until 3:00 a.m. about literally everything: philosophy and metaphysics and business and how the world works. We realized that night why the two of us had clicked immediately; we were both really passionate guys who wanted to do something exciting, something different with our lives. Neither one of us wanted to follow any of the tired old paths we were being encouraged to travel by tired old people. Neither one of us wanted to follow rules; we wanted to write our own. That evening, fueled by booze and banter, Pete and I wrote a simple business plan for an idea we had for a new website we called THAZOO.com. Pete and I had noticed that kids at UMass never seemed to know where parties were going to be on any given night. THAZOO.com would be a place where people could post information about parties and other social gatherings and other people could comment, RSVP, post pictures, and the like. (Sound familiar? Yes, this was before MySpace or Facebook.) We had no computer programming experience or money, but we were determined to find a way to make it happen.

The next morning, I started to think—really think—about my decision to join the military. Perhaps I'd jumped the gun. Don't get me wrong. I had made a commitment and was resolved to go and serve my country. But for the first time, I felt like I was starting to really understand what I was good at—what I was meant to do—and it occurred to me that I might be able to do more for America long term if I focused on starting businesses that provided value for society. It's like my friend Mike Donovan always says: "Ride the horse; don't whip the dog." In other words, instead of struggling to become a success doing something you're mildly proficient at but don't really care about, do what you enjoy doing. Build on your natural skills and talents. We have one shot at this whole "life" thing, so why waste a single minute of it?

With that in mind, I called my Navy recruiter and said, "I'd like to have a meeting with you and your superior officer." I met them for coffee, knowing that as we spoke, thousands of troops were shipping out—just like I was supposed to do in two weeks' time—and persuading the military that I'd made the wrong decision would be a long shot at best. Proposal for THAZOO.com in hand, I took a deep breath and launched into my pitch. What did I have to lose?

"Guys, first let me say that I'm resolved to go and I'm happy serve my country," I said, "but I really feel from the bottom of my heart that I'm just now figuring out what I was put on this earth to do." I handed my recruiting officer the business plan. "If you allow me to pursue this, I truly believe it will be better for the U.S. government in the long run because I'll be able to create companies that will generate the tax dollars we need to help pay for more submarines."

Either I argued my case exceptionally well or merely succeeded in convincing the naval officers that I was a complete and total lunatic (This 19-year-old nut job thinks he's gonna buy us submarines?!), but they agreed that yes, it would most likely be best for all involved if I was released from my obligation.

With the military and college checked off my list, you might think my next gig was flipping Big Macs. But I was officially beyond even attempting to believe my guidance counselor's grim counsel. Now that I knew which direction I wanted to go in, I was ready to finally move forward with purpose. I had a major epiphany, one that would shape the course of the rest of my life: It's up to us as individuals to design our own futures. If we fail to do this, not only are we squandering our potential, we're running the risk of having our lives hijacked by the intentions and demands of others.

Pete and I were all fired up about THAZOO .com, but as I mentioned, we lacked startup capital. Uncle Brian, who was in the process of building his aforementioned muscle car restoration company, did not. So to make ends meet, I spent mornings working with Brian to launch E-Muscle (the name came from the company's origins as an online muscle car parts retailer) and afternoons at Pete's house brainstorming ways to get THAZOO.com off the ground.

E-Muscle proved the perfect training ground for a fledgling entrepreneur like myself. Because my uncle was all about nuts and bolts, it was essentially up to me to create a lot of the infrastructure for the business. E-Muscle gave me the chance to employ my skills in creating a brand for the first time by figuring out ways to market my uncle's relatively simple idea—"I want to restore muscle cars"—as one of the most in-demand services of its kind. The first change I made in company policy was to get rid of our advertising budget. Instead of wasting money on traditional ads, I thought we could attract the same level of attention for free by sending out well-crafted, timely press releases and cultivating relationships with journalists. It was here that I started to learn the subtle art of managing the media and creating buzz, and how to have fun doing it; one of the most exciting memories I have of this time was when my uncle was featured on Spike TV for restoring one of the world's rarest muscle cars. Together, Uncle Brian and I grew E-Muscle into a multimillion-dollar restoration shop, bringing in rare cars from all over the world. Meanwhile, Pete and I were hard at work promoting THAZOO.com. As is often the case with new ventures, we found ourselves going down a different course than originally intended. As a way to raise capital, we started throwing parties—and soon realized that throwing parties was a profitable venture all its own. So the social media aspect of THAZOO.com didn't really happen (a development we'd momentarily kick ourselves over when MySpace and Facebook exploded on the scene), but our new direction took us exactly where we needed to be. The thing is, Pete and I threw great parties— the sort of hip, over-the-top events one might attend regularly in New York City but rarely in our corner of Connecticut. Word traveled fast, and soon, high-profile types were seeking us out, music industry professionals in particular. Our big break came when Jay-Z and Jagged Edge rolled into Hartford for a concert at the Civic Center and their managers asked us to throw the official after party. The event was a huge success and catapulted us into the territory of full-time promoters.

Pete and I both liked to party, of course, and were equally passionate about music (I played drums for years), so there were worse gigs than hosting sexy soirees for rock stars, as far as we were concerned. Still, we were itching to do something more—and within a couple of years, we knew exactly what that something more should be.

With the number of major recording acts coming through Connecticut—being strategically located between New York City and Boston—what our home state really needed was a high-quality, well-respected recording studio. Sure, there were plenty of top-notch studios in the Big Apple and Massachusetts, but we didn't feel like there were any in our own backyard that could legitimately compete with what the rest of New England had to offer. And with that, Onyx Soundlab was born. My lovely then-girlfriend, now-wife, Regina, can be credited with thinking up the "onyx" moniker (but more on that later).

Going back to Uncle Brian's credo—anything worth doing is worth doing well—we custom built the studio, paying extremely close attention to details most of our competitors missed, even down to the floors. Both Pete and I thought that beautiful pine floors would give the control room and the producer's lounge the elegant, luxurious feel we were trying to achieve. There were also acoustic benefits to pine flooring. The only problem was that we were on an extremely tight budget and the floors we wanted would have cost an extra $20,000 to install—money we didn't have. What we did have was access to a sawmill. On the centuries-old Kowalczyk family farm in Wethersfield, Pete's father had a circular blade that was about 10 feet wide and as many feet high, hooked up with a belt to the front of a 1950s pickup truck with no back end. He would turn the motor on and the belt would spin the jagged edged saw. It was one of the most horrifying sights I'd ever seen, like a particularly gory accident waiting to happen. Pete and I put our fears of becoming permanently disfigured aside and used a chainsaw to cut down a huge pine tree on the property. We then trimmed the tree and dragged it across the farm with a tractor, somehow managing to hoist it up on to the mill. The planks we sawed were of varying thicknesses, so we hand-planed every piece and hauled them down to the basement to dry for a season. The next season, despite neither one of us ever having built so much as a tree house, we taught ourselves how to make tongue-in-groove joints and installed the floors ourselves.

It was, without question, the most arduous task I've ever completed. Still, every time a client would ask, wide-eyed, "Who did these gorgeous floors?" I knew our efforts hadn't been in vain. We wanted exquisite, custom-made pine floors, and we got them. Initially, Onyx Soundlab served as a place for us to host VIPs when they were in the area. The initial feedback we got was so positive, however, that we decided we could probably make a lot more money if we opened it up to the public. One of the first things we decided to do was to double our price. At the time, competitive studios charged about $50 to $75 per hour. The week we bumped up our prices—$100 to $125 per hour—we were booked solid. It was our first real-world lesson in strategic pricing and perceived value. Simply put, most people are completely unaware of the true cost of production for whatever product or services they're purchasing. While you might think that the lowest prices will bring in the most customers, the opposite is often true: Higher prices create a greater "perceived value," making people think that whatever it is they're buying is worth the money. Of course, it goes without saying that if you're going to charge more, you need to deliver more, and we made sure to justify our prices with the best possible quality and customer service. We invested in top-of-the-line equipment and surrounded ourselves with exceptionally talented songwriters and producers. We nearly broke our backs installing those pine floors. Most important, we showered our clients with attention, making sure that every job got done exceptionally well and that the process was a blast for all involved. Our obsession with customer service began the second the phone rang. Rather than just rattle off services and hourly rates to prospective clients, we immediately started asking questions about their projects and needs: What could we do for them? It was a very effective tactic. Over the course of six years, we worked with everyone from network television to large film studios to Fortune 500 companies. Onyx Soundlab was every bit as successful as we'd hoped it would be when we were chopping down that pine tree—and then some.

But it still wasn't enough. For one thing, Pete and I became frustrated that when we weren't billing hours, we weren't making money. In order for us to bring in revenue, we had to physically be at the studio, pulling levers and twisting knobs; when we went home at night, the faucet turned off. The business model of a recording studio, particularly with the music industry in a state of digitally induced flux, would never work on a grand scale. What could we do next?

And so, we were back at the fun part. We brain-stormed for months, flirting with different concepts that got us excited. Having been committed to the concept of sustainable business concepts for years, we briefly pursued the manufacturing or import of solar panels. But this industry started feeling saturated fast. More important to us than anything was staying true to that concept of doing what we loved and creating a world for ourselves based on those passions. Solar panels were interesting, but neither one of us could claim to be over-the-top, I-can't-sleep-at-night passionate about energy.

Then, suddenly, a lightning bolt of inspiration struck. Pete and I, for reasons neither one of us can fully remember or explain, had always used the term *moonshiners* as our official production tag in the studio; it was our music industry nickname (we were credited as "The Moonshiners" on the albums we recorded). One day in 2010, I was sitting in the control room when Pete walked in and said, "Why don't we just make actual moonshine—and be the first to do it legally?"

You've probably read books where chapters end with a brilliant quote full of wisdom and inspiration. Because no great poem was ever written by a drinker of mere water, I thought I'd share a recipe for a delicious Onyx cocktail at the end of each section. Onward ho!

Onyx Moonshine on the Rocks

2 oz. Onyx Moonshine

Serve over ice.

Classic Onyx Moonshine is made for smooth sipping. Enjoy it the same way I do, simply on the rocks.

CHAPTER 2

OVERWHELM YOUR OBSTACLES WITH PASSION

Believing in Your Dream When No One Else Will

The good news was Pete and I had figured out exactly what we wanted to do: make (legal) moonshine. The bad news was nobody else seemed to think this was a good idea—at all. Bear in mind, this was 2010. Up until about 2009, there had never really been a "legally" produced moonshine available in liquor stores, and it's a federal offense to produce moonshine at home, even if it's for your own consumption. When the recession hit and states figured out that relaxing the laws regulating distilleries would both create jobs and increase tax revenue, moonshine began making its way into mainstream culture. But this shift in public perception didn't happen overnight. The most common reactions we got when we told people we planned to make moonshine were along the lines of "What, the hooch hillbillies drink?" or "That stuff makes you go blind!" or "But you guys have all your teeth!"

What the majority of people didn't—and don't—realize, however, is that most of these clichés apply to moonshine from Southern states. The Northeast has its own rich tradition of "white lightning" production and, as it turned out, both my family and Pete's had longstanding ties to this tradition.

Pete and I come from families firmly rooted in New England. Connecticut and Rhode Island were the only two states in the country to not completely pass the Eighteenth Amendment, responsible for introducing prohibition to the United States. Like those below the Mason–Dixon Line, New England farmers secretly used the excess grain and corn produced on their farms to make moonshine. It's a little-known fact that New Englanders have been doing it quietly for hundreds of years. From the moonshine perspective, there is a very different dynamic between Southerners and New Englanders. Down South, moonshine was often made from sugar, an inexpensive and easy-to-ferment base product that was readily available to them. Fermenting cane sugar is quick and results in quite a lot of alcohol; however, the resulting spirit can be harsh, and if you're not careful, may carry with it many of the hangover-inducing congeners that have given moonshine such a bad rap. In the South, you made moonshine to make a few shekels. The Southern economy struggled in the late 1800s into prohibition, and moonshining was often a way to keep the farm another year.

In New England, many gentleman farms hosted moonshining operations as well. With grain and corn growing so abundantly here, the resulting fermentation was a slower process that yielded a more complex final distillate. The resulting moonshine was essentially an unaged corn whiskey and was typically made in very small batches from whatever was left over from the fall harvest. These bottles might be shared with neighbors to help get through our horrid winters and most certainly created a sense of pride for the producers that drove a desire for complexity and smoothness.

So the difference often boiled down to quantity versus quality. A means of survival versus a hobby-like craft to be savored. Southerners were less painstaking in their process, and more likely to jar and sell whatever came out of their stills, even if it was more potent than potable. Hence moonshine's "make you go blind" reputation. I want to be careful here and clarify that I don't mean there weren't (and aren't) some damn fine Southern moonshines, with many families that have focused for generations on small batches of excellent product. Rather, as a general trend, Southern versus New England moonshine had different cultural and economic drivers that have constructed our own stereotypical views of what exactly American moonshine is.

When I started researching this period of New England history, I discovered that my family was arrested in 1864 for shipping legally produced moonshine (unaged whiskey) to Canada without paying the taxes on it, which, as it happens, is something the feds don't really like. This resulted in the closing of the family distillery, Chafee & Company Distillers. (Google *Chaffee & Co. v. United States*.) Somehow, the genetic inclination for the production of spirits surfaced again years later, with my great-grandfather, Jarius Charles Chafee, running Chafee's Hotel in Middletown, Connecticut. (Another prominent member of the Chaffee family, Herbert Fuller Chaffee, perished on the *Titanic* right before prohibition began. The various spellings aren't typos; the name appears both ways in historical documents.) During the years of prohibition, in the basement of the hotel was a speakeasy.

Meanwhile, on the Kowalczyk family farm in New Britain, Pete's great-grandmother had a secret riser in the stairway of her apartment building where people left money in the morning and picked up a flask of whiskey in the afternoon. Nutmeg State spirits practically ran in our veins. Digging further into our family histories felt like an almost spiritual confirmation that we were on the right track. It also served to broaden our mission, in a way. Now Pete and I felt a responsibility to our home state, and to tell the story of New England moonshine for the first time. Connecticut doesn't get a lot of national attention, other than being known as the "insurance capital of the world." Exciting, right?! It seems that people in other parts of the country only think of two things when they think of Connecticut: the super-wealthy Fairfield

County area, otherwise known as the "Gold Coast," and dairy farms. In reality, Connecticut is much more diverse, its history far more dynamic. We wanted to pay tribute to that history by giving the world not only a bona fide New England product, but an outstanding New England product. We wanted to elevate moonshine to a level nobody had ever seen before. We wanted to make moonshine taste so smooth that no one would believe it was moonshine. A moonshine that sipped like a top-shelf whiskey and mixed better than vodka. The way we saw it, moonshine had a global significance too, being the only authentic American spirit besides bourbon. As a matter of fact, some moonshine recipes are essentially bourbon without the barrel aging. It all starts with moonshine! Done right, moonshine could put the United States liquor industry on the map in a whole new way.

Our concept now included a mission, philosophy, and authentic story that allowed us to build a foundation on which the business plan, funding, strategy, and everything else could be built. By discovering our family heritage and thoroughly understanding the historical context of the business we were getting into, we were suddenly inspired by a vision that went beyond our desire to create a great business. We were now continuing a legacy, and the passion that surrounds that has helped inspire us and our team, even today. This thing is bigger than we are! When other brands launch, you sometimes get a sense that it was designed in a board room— complete with focus groups, expensive advertising agencies, and lots of MBAs in suits. The result occasionally comes off as stale and overly glossy. It can certainly be a good thing for any business to have that caliber of professionals around it to ensure success, but as I'll discuss later, consumers more and more crave true authenticity.

We would need to spend months refining our recipe and working out the kinks of the distillation process before we came close to creating a liquor that could be the very best in its category. Without the end goal of being the very top, market-leading brand in a given industry, what exactly is the point? Every brand we all know and respect at some point was a startup. And they all strove for and achieved greatness. As a result, success looked like a couple of things: financial freedom for the founders, executives, and even for the company itself to continue creating and perpetuating itself; brand respect and recognition in the eyes of consumers and media; and last, the achievement of the ultimate goal. As you create your business plan or look to grow your company, I suggest you envision yourself and what you've created placed at the very top of the market in which you'll be active. Strive to have the best customer service or create that product that will change lives in such a positive, impactful way that you're numero uno in whatever it is that you do. Be the best, period. This is a lifelong mantra worth having; take it with you into business and flourish as a result.

Alas, the first most critical step remained: We needed the funds to get started. I'm a big believer in using OPM (other people's money) for all business ventures. There is *a lot* of it out there, and they need to deploy those funds to get better returns than the bank. I'll expand on this much more in later chapters.

Pete and I were fortunate to find our first investor through a client we'd been working with at Onyx Soundlab, a talented young female singer whose father was the CEO of a major food distribution company that serviced much of New England. I have always been an advocate of connecting with good, like-minded people on the trajectory of success. In that spirit, Pete and I befriended this man. As an experienced, influential businessman, he was someone we could learn a lot from. His instincts were spot-on; he was an early investor many successful start-up brands. Personally, I was incredibly curious about what he did on a day-to-day basis and jumped at the chance when he offered to give us a tour of his facility. I'll never forget walking through that warehouse, where dozens of 18-wheelers were parked waiting for what seemed like hundreds of forklifts to fill them with food that would then be transported to grocery stores all over the Northeast. This man had built a veritable empire. I wanted to learn his secrets.

As we prepared to launch what would become Onyx Spirits Company, Pete and I considered putting together an advisory board of knowledgeable businesspeople who could give us valuable input and feedback on our ideas. I reached out to the young singer's father at that point and asked him if he would be willing to be a member. "One of the things we're hoping people on the board can do is to help us raise the initial amount of money to make this happen," I said. "How much do you need?" he asked. I knew our startup funds were not huge in the investment world by any means; nonetheless, it was a significant amount of money. "The minimum amount we need to get the first phase of this business off the ground is $150,000," I said. He replied, "Well, that's not very much. Why don't you come by next week and I'll write you a check?"

I wasn't entirely shocked by his generosity, but I was surprised at how easily our momentum developed. A natural momentum surrounding a project is a positive sign, not to be taken lightly. (I don't want to gloss over this absolutely critical piece of the venture's launch, and I will expand on investor fundraising later on.) With the initial funding in place, it was time for Pete and I to move from the conceptual, business-planning stage to mapping out our concrete operations. Neither one of us had been in manufacturing before, so this "mapping out" was uncharted territory for us. We had to learn about the nuts and bolts of everything: what sort of equipment we would need beyond just the moonshine stills, how we would systemize a repeatable process that involved bottling and labeling, and, of course, the tactical plan of selling and marketing.

Our first rookie mistake was choosing aesthetics over functionality. Sometimes, my overly romantic approach to business can be a detriment. For our base of operations, we selected a restored Civil War–era factory in Manchester, Connecticut. On paper, it was a picturesquely perfect site for a liquor distillery. The old place produced the suit for George Washington's inaugural address, and during the Civil War it made uniforms for the Union. It definitely had a cool, atmospheric vibe; I'll say that much. It would have made a great period film set—and that's about it. In our brilliant wisdom we selected a manufacturing headquarters that lacked a loading dock, high ceilings, a bathroom, and offices. The cement floor had so many ancient divots in it, you could hardly roll a pallet jack with it teetering dangerously, threatening to bury one of us under 1,000 glass bottles.

When I say Pete and I didn't know what we were doing, I mean we really didn't know what we were doing. To make matters even more complicated, distilling moonshine as a legal business in New England was such a new concept that there were very few local people we could ask for advice. Neither Pete nor I had any sort of background in science or chemistry, never mind manufacturing processes or liquor distribution experience. To compensate, we bought every book we could find on the subject and spent endless hours scouring the Internet for tips. We were lucky to make a friend, Don, an awesome older gentleman who was head of R&D for the long-closed Hartford-based Hublein Company. Hublein brought Smirnoff to the marketplace in the 1950s and was really responsible for bringing vodka to the American spirits market. Don had personally designed the formula for Yukon Jack.

I believe you can learn absolutely anything if you're motivated, and ultimately, the process we designed was straightforward enough. Besides, we'd been making plenty of batches of beer and other drinkables at home. For those of you who know nothing of how spirits our made, you start by producing a beer made from whatever your grain recipe is. We loved the flavor profile of corn and malted barley, and focused on tweaking that recipe for quite some time. Fermentation is basically using yeast to convert starches to sugars, then converting those sugars to alcohol. I don't want to get too heavily into the technical art of distilling, but there are some great books out there if you'd like to learn more. *The Craft of Whiskey Distilling* by Bill Owens is a great example. After fermentation, we heat the mash to distill out the alcohol, which separates the alcohol from the grain and passes it through a coil cooled by circulated water. The alcohol is condensed back into liquid form and then collected. I still tease our brewery owner friends that they only do half the job. Distillers take it to the finish line!

The art of distilling gets much more complicated as you begin crafting the flavor profile you desire. Many people spend their entire lives devoted to this perfect combination of science and craft, not unlike world-renowned winemakers. The product of a distillate is divided into three separate parts: the heads, hearts, and tails. Hearts, as you might have guessed, are filled with good stuff: the magical, buzz-making elixir that human beings have toasted for centuries. Heads and tails, however, are filled in part with evil stuff: the diabolical, hangover-making swill that human beings have cursed for centuries. They also have some of the key flavor components that make a spirit exceptionally delicious. Separating the good from the bad requires constant, careful monitoring of the still's temperature. With every degree point comes a new flavor—and a new side effect. The goal, naturally, is to keep the flavor and ditch the side effects. The very first liquid to drip from the still is more or less pure methanol—the stuff that really will make you go blind or even kill you. You could run your moped on it. Pete and I learned that one the hard way, using an old copper still we found on his family's farm (once we had our initial permit, of course). Although both of us still have our eyesight, those shots will go down in history as the most regrettable of our lives. All told, we made hundreds of experimental batches using a variety of different types of water. Municipal water didn't work; it gave the moonshine a strong chlorine "bouquet," if you could call it that. Regular bottled water didn't result in the taste we were shooting for, either. We finally hit the jackpot with water from a local family-owned spring.

Almost as important as developing the (now-secret) Onyx recipe was developing the Onyx brand. After getting over their initial shock at our interest in doing moonshine, nearly everyone who heard what we were up to gave us the same suggestions, like "Hey, why don't you sell it in mason jars?" or "You should put an old racecar/guy in a straw hat on the label." No one's ideas were in keeping with our concept of making a moonshine that was respectable and exuded high-end quality. Our mission was to create a bottle that would look at home on the top shelf of any bar, not a package that would scare potential drinkers away with backwoods stereotypes. Plus, pouring from a mason jar would pose a serious problem for bartenders from a mixing standpoint, with valuable product spilling all over the place. We went with a relatively safe bottle, a classic, tapered shape with a thick glass base—one that made a satisfying thud when you set it down. Instead of the increasingly popular screw top, we chose a wooden cork to add an organic earthiness into the mix and create an enjoyable sensory *plunk* when you uncork it. When designing any product, a lot of thought should be spent on designing the aesthetics of the entire experience. As I type this right now, the solid click of Apple's MacBook Air sounds and feels nicer than any other laptop I've ever typed on. They obviously put some real engineering into the springs or whatever lies beneath the little keys I peck around on. Mercedes actually has in-house acoustic programs that design the vault-like sound when you close the door. If you've ever been in a Mercedes, you may have noticed the reassuringly soundproof experience that ensures you that all is safe and you're riding in luxury. We needed to create a full experience with our bottle before it even reaches the lips of the consumer to convey in advance the quality that awaits within.

As for the label design, that was a journey all its own. We spent more than six months revising the design with a team of graphic artists, obsessing over the smallest details. I was determined to get it just right. There were so many messages we wanted to convey with the Onyx label: Luxury, elegance, and accessibility were keywords. Sprinkle in a hint of the Old World to harken back to our history and that of moonshine. We made collages of pictures cut out from magazines to inspire us. There were snippets of Louis Vuitton ads, photos of old saloon signs, and my favorite car, a black 1956 Jaguar Roadster with its smooth, sexy lines. We also included our state symbol, the Charter Oak, so that no matter how big Onyx got, no one would ever forget it came from Connecticut. Finally, we chose colors that were striking and classic: gold, white, and of course, onyx black.

This brings us to the name, Onyx. We always say that the true origin of our name is a secret—much like our recipe—but I'll reveal this much. Onyx, as a gemstone, embodies many of the characteristics Pete and I hoped to achieve with both Onyx Soundlab and Onyx Spirits Company. Onyx is high quality but not pretentious, bold but understated. All with a sprinkle of that mystical, Tim Burton-esque gothic sensibility I personally love as an added stylistic bonus.

Pete and I were completely committed to our vision of perfecting the world's first premium moonshine but, as I mentioned, not everyone had faith in the idea—including our investor. Don't get me wrong; he had faith in us as entrepreneurs, even as distillers. He just happened to be of the opinion that we should be producing vodka or limoncello instead of moonshine. As a matter of fact, we were producing all three. But whereas our investor thought of the vodka and limoncello as our main offerings, Pete and I thought of them as backups. Think about it: The vodka aisle at every liquor store is a million miles long. Even if we made the most amazing vodka in the world, how much demand was there for yet another take on the colorless Russian liquor? Especially without the huge capital needed to usurp established brands with billions of dollars behind them. We knew we were working with a very small budget and as a result had to create a new niche in a new category, with a new brand. Not a small challenge, but at least we wouldn't be lost in the sauce. Would a vodka capture the minds of the media and score us some free PR? Likely not. No free PR means we would have had to pay for advertising, which was really not in the budget. I read the other day that advertising is a tax you pay for not being remarkable. God, I love that quote! We made an absolutely amazing version of the lemon-flavored liqueur, if I do say so myself, but it would never sell the way we hoped our moonshine would. Why? Our market research showed us that consumers in the United States consume limoncello once, maybe twice per year. We needed to be a weekly, go-to, after-work cocktail option for our customers. Plus, zesting lemons really sucks and there's no machine designed that can remove the zest without taking the pith with it, which is the key to a good limoncello. (Hmm, potential business idea?)

Then, fate intervened. About a month before we were ready to launch our vodka and limoncello, another local company (funded by an investor who didn't return our call) beat us to the punch. Plus, the name we'd chosen for our vodka was being challenged by a big company. When Pete and I heard the news, we were at the distillery. We looked around at the cases of empty glass bottles, the shiny copper stills and stacked barrels of booze, and the crates of lemons we brought in. There was no room in the local market for another brand of limoncello, we were certain of that.

"What do we do?" asked Pete.

"We go back to our original plan," I said. "Let's make the best damn moonshine America has ever seen."

Our investor was more than a little surprised by our decision. I believe his exact words were, "Why didn't you tell me?!" But it didn't take long for his borderline dismay to evolve into a more positive outlook. Within a month, we'd sold our estimate for a year in sales: 5,000 bottles.

Our immediate success so far exceeded our initial expectations that we were over the moon (pardon the almost pun). We were also, for better or worse, overextended almost from the moment of our very first order. Stefan, the manager of Maximum

Beverage in West Hartford, Connecticut, rang us up and said, "Hey, I've been getting a bunch of calls from people about your moonshine. Can I order a couple of cases?" Running on sheer adrenaline, Pete and I loaded up the trunk of my car (just like back in the days of my Great Candy Caper) and drove straight to the store. A couple of hours later, the phone rang again. "Hey, it's all gone! Can you bring us a couple more cases?" The third time we went to Maximum Beverage that day, we brought 10 cases. The next day, the owner called back. "We're sold out again."

That's when Onyx Spirits Company officially exploded. My voice mail filled up continually with messages from retailers trying to get their hands on our product. Pete and I spent the next four months delivering moonshine as fast as we could make it. We were constantly filling and emptying the trunk of my car, driving to liquor stores all over New England. It's safe to say we were in shock. As amazing and wonderful as it is when a company starts to take off, there's a certain kind of chaos that occurs: Demand skyrockets so high you can't keep up with it; customers are unhappy because they're not getting the product on time;

press opportunities are missed because you're too busy to make appearances or give interviews. At that point, we realized that we needed to learn how to delegate. The business was running us instead of vice versa. We started by appointing a distributor for Connecticut, Allan S. Goodman. Connecticut is a three-tier state, which means alcohol suppliers can only sell to wholesale distributors, who then sell to retailers, and only retailers can sell to consumers. Every single distributor in the area called us within weeks of Onyx going to market; they all wanted meetings based on the calls *they* were getting from their sales guys about this new moonshine nobody could keep in stock. Why was Onyx selling so well? Ultimately, because people liked our product—but there were also a few sales tactics I'd employed that proved extremely effective.

My first strategy involved in-store advertising, so to speak. Not only would I give retailers Onyx posters and shelf-talkers, I would also give them the following spiel: "Do us a favor and leave one bottle on the counter. When customers realize you're one of the stores around here that carries Onyx, it'll fly off the shelves." Now, common sense dictates that anything you put on the front counter is bound to sell more. So naturally, when shop owners complied (which they almost always did), Onyx actually did fly off the shelves. In essence, we got priority placement of our product by suggesting the obvious, phrased in a way that pointed out the benefit to them. To date, I've never seen a product placed on a front counter consistently for a period of time. I have a feeling it's because no one has thought to ask! Speaking of shelves, my next tactic had to do with shelf placement. I felt very strongly against stores putting Onyx next to the vodka, the reason being that vodka drinkers have been so programmed toward flavorless alcohol that they're going to shy away from anything with character. We identified more with Jack Daniels. Plus, Jack Daniels' popularity meant that it was usually placed at eye level in the middle of the store. Other local, craft distillers often asked to be placed in the "Connecticut" or boutique section, but we knew the highest traffic section was the place to be. So when retailers asked us where they should stock Onyx, we never hesitated: It goes quite well with Jack. As a matter of fact, some customers will leave with a bottle of Onyx *and* a bottle of Jack Daniels.

We took a similarly calculated approach to determining a price point. The recession was barely behind us when Onyx launched, and we wanted to make it an affordable luxury, something regular working-class families would be able to enjoy. We settled on a $25 per bottle retail price: lower than most super-premium spirits and small production craft spirits, and higher than standard everyday well drinks. We also did a lot of analysis regarding our pricing to fully understand the market. Keep in mind, too, that because each state has different liquor excise taxes, and in different markets distributors and retailers expect different margins as their standard, we had to be sensitive about future growth and how our margins would be affected. It's a somewhat-complicated formula that is always changing. We did research. Lots of it. Obviously, in our market analysis we needed to gain a thorough understanding of what other brands look like and how they're performing, who their customer is, and their wholesale and retail pricing strategy.

Ultimately, we felt $24.99 was a pricing sweet spot—sandwiched below super-premium brands like Grey Goose, far above well brands like Smirnoff, and about a buck or two lower than

Jack Daniels. I like to refer to all of these different methods as "guerrilla tactics" because when it comes down to it, Onyx is a guerrilla company—a little group of rebels taking on giant corporations like Diageo and Bacardi and occasionally outselling their products. When Onyx Moonshine became the 20th top-selling spirit in the state of Connecticut for our distributors, my friend and mentor Mike Donovan, vice president at Allan S. Goodman and a 30-year liquor industry veteran, said something to me I'll never forget: "I've never seen a brand do this."

And to think, if we made vodka or limoncello like everybody wanted us to, none of this ever would have happened.

Apple Cider Old-Fashioned

1 1/2 oz. Secret Stash Reserve Whiskey
3 oz. hard apple cider
1/2 oz. sweet vermouth
1/2 oz. honey

Garnish with brandied cherries and/or orange slices.

John Adams was known to imbibe a gill (3 to 4 ounces) of hard cider every day at breakfast. The iconic New England flavors mixed into this classic whiskey cocktail brings old and new together.

⁓ CHAPTER 3 ⁓

FIND YOUR PETER

*Surrounding Yourself With People Who
Support Your Strengths (and Make Up
for Your Weaknesses)*

Although the initial success of Onyx can be partly attributed to our disregard for certain people's opinions (particularly regarding our choice of spirit), the company wouldn't have continued to grow if we hadn't paid close attention to the counsel of others. The thing is, nearly everybody you'll meet in business (and life) has something valuable to teach you, even if it's simply what not to do.

I learned pretty quickly that one of the most important factors in deciding if someone is worth listening to is whether or not that individual has created a life that inspires you and that you would like to replicate. If you learn from someone you deem successful, they have a formula they've employed. In the formula are tons of little lessons you can take and apply to your own model of business or life. Take my Uncle Bob, for example. Interestingly, he was one of the many people to raise an incredulous eyebrow at the idea of making moonshine in the first place, but even if he didn't quite understand my vision, he was still right there with exactly the words of wisdom I needed whenever some new challenge presented itself. And believe me: Challenges presented themselves often. I should mention that, now, he's probably our biggest customer and totes Onyx to all corners of the globe for people to try. One example of some much-needed wisdom came after we were months behind on our initial release target date. Several factors contributed to the delay. We suffered setbacks with label approval on a federal level, and local red tape held up production authorization. Meanwhile, we'd been teasing the launch of Onyx for nearly a year on social media and with prospective retailers and bartenders. I went to Uncle Bob in a panic over the fact that we weren't meeting our self-imposed deadlines. If there is a philosophy we try to live by consistently with our businesses, it is to underpromise and over-deliver. One of the gravest mistakes we could make as a fledgling company, we were told, would be to tell consumers we were going to do something and then *not* do it. Uncle Bob understood my fears, but he had a different, equally valuable perspective to offer: "Think about it," he said. "When companies like Microsoft and Apple release a new product, they start talking about it two years in advance. By the time whatever it is comes out, people are buzzing about it. Get people talking. That's more important than making some deadline."

He was right. That particular kind of powerful, built-over-time buzz can't be bought for any amount of advertising dollars, something we relearned a couple of years later when we launched Onyx Secret Stash, Connecticut's first barrel-aged whiskey, released in conjunction with the 80th anniversary of the repeal of prohibition. We started promoting Secret Stash on Facebook and Twitter a good nine months before it hit the shelves; when it did, we sold out almost immediately: almost two thousand bottles at $70 a pop. There are a couple reasons why this was such a big win. First, we were able to sell the product *in advance* to the distributors based on the buzz around the product. That meant we got paid six months in advance. Because we created such fervent pull on the retailer side, the retailers didn't sit on it for long. Retailers love turnover. So we got paid fast, created tons of publicity, and pulled the product right through the retailers to the happy, whiskey-drinking consumers. Everyone won. Some business lessons transcend whatever industry you happen to be in, which is why my uncle's voice of experience proved priceless despite the fact that he had no background in liquor. Other things, however, we would need to learn from die-hard liquor biz veterans.

As I mentioned in the last chapter, things became almost intolerably—if amazingly—crazy for Pete and me when Onyx started getting really popular. After four months of frantically delivering cases of moonshine out of the trunk of my car, it became clear that we were no longer running the business; the business was running us. Thanks to reports from sales reps and retailers of our product disappearing from stores shelves, distributors were calling us every day, multiple times a day, trying to set up meetings—meetings we were too busy to make because we were so swamped making and transporting moonshine. We thought about getting a truck and hiring a driver, but we didn't want to be in the business of delivering. We wanted to be in the business of creating a quality product and spreading the gospel of that product. Our only choice was to find the time to meet with one of the distributors courting us, but the question was, which one? One of the trickiest aspects of the liquor business is choosing the right distributor. I imagine this is the case for many industries; unfortunately, many spirit distributors get a bad rap for partnering up with small brands, making big promises, and not delivering, exactly what we'd been warned against doing ourselves. Part of the reason for this is because many distributors are beholden to much larger brands that bring in the majority of their cash flow. Sure, they might have every intention of following through on their pledge to get your product into a certain number of stores, but at the end of the day, if Diageo calls up and says, "Hey, we've got this great new whipped cream/marshmallow/salmon-flavored vodka we want you to get placed into stores stat," guess which company that distributor is going to focus their attention on? Not your underfunded craft distillery, that's for sure.

Pete and I wanted to avoid becoming one of these overlooked industry casualties, so we went out and asked retailers and everybody else we could think of in the trade: Who's your favorite distributor to work with? Are they fair? Are they reliable?

Everyone we came in contact with spoke very highly of distributors Allan S. Goodman. Beyond their glowing reputation, we decided to sign with them for a couple of different reasons. First of all, as the exclusive distributors of Jack Daniels in Connecticut, they're major players. Literally every single bar, restaurant, and liquor store in the state has an account with Allan S. Goodman because every single account has to sell Jack Daniels. Second, even though they're "big time," Allan S. Goodman is still local in their mindset and approach. They're family-owned and operated, and have been since the day they opened, which funnily enough was the day after prohibition ended. In my opinion they think big, but act small. Our instincts turned out to be right on the money, literally. Allan S. Goodman's vice president, Mike Donovan, has been critical in saving us time and funds by helping us to avoid some of the most common mistakes made by fledgling brands—and with

30 years of spirits-world experience behind him, he's seen them all.

We needed his help in a major way. The first time we met with him, he asked me how many off-premise and on-premise accounts we had. I had no idea what he was talking about; those terms were entirely unknown to me. I soon found out those were examples of standard industry lingo for liquor stores (or, as we say in New England, package stores) and restaurants. This was the first of many lessons we learned from Mike. Pete and I now had a decent understanding of how things worked in our chosen field, but we still didn't fully grasp the complexities of signing with a distributor when we first met with Mike. There was nowhere to go to really learn about this ahead of time, and part of the challenge is each state and market is segmented pretty differently in the spirits business. Teaming up with Goodman meant tacking some pretty significant costs on to our bottom line, costs that would cut directly into our net profit. We really had to make the decision as to whether or not we wanted to be producers or distributors: If we were to continue to internalize our distribution method, we'd have to expand it. That meant buying and maintaining trucks, and the liability of having employees behind the wheel, not to mention still needing to have someone doing some sales time with key accounts. When we realized just how much moonshine we would need to sell to offset these costs, Pete and I started to worry. Thankfully, we had Mike there to show us the ropes, and we decided to let distributors do what they do best so we could focus on the core of the business. See, when big companies like Diageo introduce a new product, they spend tremendous amounts of money on advertising and other gimmicks to drill the existence of that new whipped cream/marshmallow/salmon-flavored vodka into people's heads. Because such big-budget methods weren't possible for us, we had to focus on getting customers behind our brand in different ways—the aforementioned guerrilla tactics of courting the press, generating buzz via social media, and throwing over-the-top promotional events. Basically, the difference can be explained thusly: We built our brand from the bottom up, not from the top down. We created genuine *pull* in the marketplace, as opposed to *pushing* our product on customers. Essentially, by not copying the standard model of how spirits are produced, and by obsessing over the actual customer's wants, we forged a whole new model for releasing a spirit brand, and it's that very model that's allowed us to compete with so many capitalized, entrenched brands. With limited resources, we had no choice but to approach the market the way we did—and ended up building a more solid foundation than many better-capitalized startups do in the process. Plus, we've been forced to remember, at every stage of the game, that the point is to give consumers the best possible product in any given category— something bigger companies tend to forget. In fact, refining our "push versus pull" strategy only served to intensify Onyx's long-standing obsession with consumer experience.

I believe that the difference between a business that's going to succeed in the long run is one that has focused on the customer to such an extent that the natural pull through on the customer side will allow the company to overcome just about any obstacles that will arise. By creating a product the customer truly wants—not one you think they want—and doing every single thing in your power to ensure they know about you, you will build a real business. The business will have roots that go deep, and it will be harder to topple during the inevitable little storms that will come. I mentioned before that every distributor in the area was coming to us and asking to distribute our moonshine. We had our choice of distributors and were able to negotiate good terms because we had pull. We were able to leverage customer pull for good strategic partners that helped us grow further, and that pull attracted some really talented staff. Pull made our retailers happy with our brand and excited to sell it. Without pull, we would have had to approach distributors and say, "We would like to explore distribution options with you." They have hundreds of brands and might have said they weren't interested because they'd realize we'd have no organic pull, so they'd have to invest substantial resources to get the brand moving units. Having real pull then gave us great sales numbers, which in turn we have been able to use as a critical asset in attracting more investors for growth capital. I can't stress this enough: Pull is everything.

Signing with a distributor allowed us to amplify our efforts in ways we never dreamed possible. Allan S. Goodman has 40 to 50 sales reps pounding the pavement every day, each one carrying a book filled with hundreds of products. They also have relationships with important national distributors and the incredibly useful ability to help us make those connections. Again, the knowledge and expertise we gained—and continue to gain from teaming up with our distributor, and from Mike Donovan in particular—could only be acquired from spirits industry veterans. You cannot beat the value of adding someone to your advisory team who knows what the hell they're doing, and I have vowed to never underestimate this again. Still, we've also learned the importance of maintaining diversity in the people you choose to learn from—and work with—on a day-to-day basis. Take our first major investor, the food distribution company CEO. He's extremely successful, like I said, but not a beverage industry guy—and a bit less of an entrepreneur than a practical, efficient company leader with a significantly more conservative approach than my own. CEOs and entrepreneurs are rarely the same types of folks and often have different risk thresholds. Being at the helm of an established, massive operation like the one he runs, his priorities—rightly so—is profitability and protecting the company. Whenever Pete and I get caught up in the details of creating our infrastructure or the details of our next big idea, he's there to remind us: "Look, I know you guys have a vision, but don't forget that without money, that vision will never become a reality." He reminds us to manage our costs and has shown us on more than one occasion that profitability isn't always about selling more; sometimes, it's about unique, creative ways to lower costs in unexpected places. It still amazes me how much money can be found simply by managing costs better. After one of our meetings with our investor, I was so inspired to cut costs, I called up our spring water supplier. I told them we were looking at a competitor and we needed them to lower our price 20%. Precisely two minutes later they said yes and we hung up. Wow, that was easy. I had never thought to just call a supplier and ask for a lower price. There was an immediate effect on our cash flow as a result, and we expanded our margins. Wham, bam.

And although food distribution isn't so far removed from our own profession, it's worth noting that we've been fortunate to find guidance from experts in completely unrelated fields. My good friend Michael Polo, president of aerospace firm AdChem Manufacturing Technologies, designs high-level components for government tanks and airplanes and has saved us thousands of potential dollars, not only by introducing us to the concept of lean product, but also by assigning some of his staff to help consult us on it, for free. If you're not familiar with lean production, it was brilliantly designed by Toyota as a means of eliminating waste in manufacturing. We embraced simple suggestions like moving a table on the assembly line across the room to knock off 5 cents per bottle. Having a friend advisor that is experienced in lean manufacturing and the philosophy centered on preserving value with less work is a great example of how asking friends, embracing change, and a focus on constant improvement can have direct impacts on your costs and bottom line. Pete and I quickly learned to appreciate the value of these fresh perspectives, which kept us from getting boxed into a traditional liquor industry mentality—an appreciation that influences our hiring practices to this day. To work at Onyx, an employee doesn't always need experience in the spirits business, although they must be passionate about liquor (particularly our products). One of the best examples of how this concept has worked in our favor is Deb

Coggshall. We discovered Deb on a company-sponsored team and asked her to join our official tasting team, made up of passionate Onyx moonshine drinkers. We loved her energy and enthusiasm so much that before long, we asked her to represent Onyx at in-store tasting events. Now, as anyone who's ever sampled lukewarm chardonnay from a plastic cup knows, the industry standard for in-store tastings is to hire a hot girl with, shall we say, "limited communication skills," who generally knows nothing about the product she's supposed to be promoting and spends more time looking at her smartphone than she does talking up boozery. Deb, on the other hand, knows our brand almost as well as we do. She's even worked the bottling line, so she can say she's truly had a hand in helping to make Onyx, and she consistently breaks records, once selling 40 bottles in two hours. Deb has become such an asset to our company, and allowing her to flourish and embrace her talent has resulted in record-breaking sales, more customers, and happy retailers. All of this, with no prior liquor industry experience whatsoever. To me, more important than anything on a potential employee's résumé is what you see in their eyes. Is there a spark? Is this person a vibrant part of the universe? Are they genuinely excited about your company's mission? Do they exude all things above mediocrity? If the answer to any of these questions is no, you're better off moving on to the next candidate.

Of course, all the wise mentors, like-minded colleagues, and loyal employees in the world would mean nothing if I didn't have the ideal business partner—for me, anyway. That's the thing with Pete and me: Our dynamic is such that we each make up for what the other lacks, which in my opinion is exactly the dynamic every startup entrepreneur should look for in a partnership, if you're entering into one. In our case, I'm the extrovert and Pete is the introvert. I'm creative and tend to be an optimist; I'm always full of big, crazy (occasionally stupid) ideas; Pete is more of a practical type who'll take my big, crazy ideas and analyze the hell out of them, pointing out all the challenges. My spirits are recharged from interacting with the press and customers; Pete leaves big events feeling drained. Because of our differences, we realized very early on that the smartest decision we could make as partners would be to divide the business in half, so to speak, with each of us playing very clearly defined roles: Pete manages the books and oversees production and general back office operations management while I manage sales, distribution, and marketing. There's an element of good cop/bad cop to the way we work, as well. People tend to think of me as "the friendly one"—the guy who's likely to end a meeting with a big hug. In the business world, I've been mistaken for someone who can be out-negotiated. Pete, on the other hand, with his glassy blue eyes and reserved demeanor, can be a pretty intimidating dude when he has to be. As a man of few words, when he actually speaks up, people listen—and more often than not, their response is "Whoa. We better not mess with him!"

Individually, I'm not sure Pete or I could do what we do on a daily basis—but together, we're a force to be reckoned with. But that's not even the best part about finding the right business partner. The best part about finding the right partner is that you have someone to share the weight of your responsibilities. I hear a lot of stories from people who had the misfortune of getting into tough business partnerships—decades-long friendships destroyed by one failed coffee shop or boutique bread bakery. It's a shame and, in my opinion, something that can be avoided by following a few basic ground rules. Here's what I've learned from my years of working with Pete about founding a business partnership that's built to last:

- Communication is key. Right from the start, be open and honest. Talk everything through, from tiny, seemingly insignificant matters to life-changing decisions. And sometimes, you should hang out and get drunk.
- Define your roles clearly—and early. As with Pete and me, assign duties based on personal strengths and individual talents. Go with your gut. Remember that you're there to fill in each other's blanks whenever possible.
- Don't start a business on a handshake. A clear-cut operating agreement clarifying everything from sharing expenses and profits to length of commitment will save you serious headaches—not to mention potential heartache. This is an area where you should not skimp on the legal fees.

- Only go into business with someone you know very, very well. The truth is, not everyone is cut out for the hard work and struggle that come with starting a new venture. If both you and your partner are motivated by the same things—in the case of Pete and me, the ability to create new and exciting products—you'll be more likely to tough it out through the hard times and stick around for the long haul.

Give some long, hard thought to the kind of person you are and to who you business partner truly is. It can be a real rarity to find a business person you can build with for the long haul. They can say that to truly understand one's character, you have to see who they become in the face of difficulty and challenge. If you don't know the answer, you're probably not ready to engage in a serious business decision.

From the beginning, Pete and I made a decision: There was no other option but success. No backup plan, no safety net, no going back. And because of that shared mindset, we've remained 110 percent committed. This is not to say that we don't sometimes have creative differences; we've just found ways to deal with them. When we get into a really heated debate, for example, we occasionally role play; we each argue the other person's point of view for a few minutes. Interestingly, 99 percent of the time, we end up meeting each other halfway—and with a solution or an idea that's exponentially better than what either one of us had in the beginning.

I've been asked by investors (and curious folk) who makes the *final* call when Pete and I are at a stalemate. I entirely understand the question, and I'd want to know the same. The numbers show that any two humans together will invariably have a disagreement. Business can be an emotional thing, and your investors will want to see a chain of command that makes them feel comfortable and fits inside their neat little boxy worldview of law and order. That being said, we've never had a stalemate. I firmly believe that if you truly understand someone and are coming from the same place of goodness and an interest in mutual benefit and progress, you can work hard to see each other's point of view and come out with a strong solution. Try it next time your spouse argues with you! By recognizing that you benefit more as one unit, work to see their point of view, and help them to see yours. It's truly a magical, wisdom-filled, almost Buddhist way to "argue." Then everyone leaves the conversation feeling all sorts of warm and fuzzy.

Voilà. That's what finding your Peter is all about.

P.S. Pete didn't like me calling this chapter "Finding Your Peter." I on the other hand, am thoroughly amused. Therefore, my last piece of advice on this topic is: You both best have an awesome sense of humor. Laugh much. Otherwise, what's the point?

The Bee's Knees

1 1/2 oz. Onyx Moonshine
1/2 oz. orange juice
1/4 oz. lemon juice
1 tsp. honey or honey simple syrup

Shake and pour on the rocks.

The Bee's Knees was one of America's very first cocktails, designed during prohibition to mask the flavors of poorly produced moonshines of the 1920s and 1930s.

CHAPTER 4

CHASE THE INSATIABLE HORIZON

The Art of Setting—and Reaching—Your Goals

If having a similar mindset as your business partner (or partners) is the first building block to success, it could be said that developing a shared philosophy is the next—and perhaps most crucial—step. In fact, developing a singular guiding principle for your venture is just as important for solo entrepreneurs. Early on in our partnership, Pete and I came up with a concept that would become the main defining principle of not just our business but our lives: the insatiable horizon. "What exactly is an insatiable horizon?" you ponder, intrigued and sweating with the suspense? Well, there are positive insatiable horizons and negative insatiable horizons, but more on that in a minute.

The insatiable horizon, by nature, holds an untold amount of life-changing promise. As we define it, the insatiable horizon is the inevitable life-goal destinations we create in our heads that allow us to keep some level of sanity and to continue pushing forward every day. It is that something the average person spends his or her entire existence running toward—a goal that's forever changing, sometimes unattainable, like a dangling carrot that always manages to be just out of reach. You know exactly what I'm talking about: *If I just close this deal, I'd have my financial problems fixed. If I could just get funding, we'd change the world. If my neighbor would just stop feeding the birds, I could sleep at night without vexatious bird crap all over my car in the morning.* Humanity needs something to reach for on the horizon, and it's an insatiable hunger because we always want more. Actually, being truly happy with what you have can take quite a bit of mental work and meditation. Now, devoting oneself to the pursuit of the unattainable can be considered a beneficial approach to life: The very definition of insatiable—impossible to satisfy—implies a perennial hunger, an endless thirst for more that, at best, safeguards against the kind of complacency responsible for keeping less-driven types stuck in dead-end jobs for decades. So it's a good thing that humans have a natural inclination to create insatiable horizons for themselves. The problem is that when they finally arrive at their chosen destination, so to speak, they often find that still further away in the distance is a new insatiable horizon. Think of it as a "grass is always greener" mindset that eternally perpetuates itself. That's why it's so important to remember that achieving a goal isn't just about the goal itself. It's about whom you become on the journey to that coveted end result. It's about the character built in the process. And finally, it's about always remaining conscious of where you want to go next.

In a way, you could say that the first insatiable horizon Pete and I set for Onyx (after conceiving of the idea for the company and the subsequent plan of action, of course) was finding the perfect location to launch our fledgling business. After much searching, we chose a 2,000-square-foot space in Manchester, Connecticut. The insatiable horizon spoke to us like this: *If only we had an amazing place to make it in, then we'd have the foundation for success!* Beyond its relative afford-ability and proximity to our homes, Pete and I were sold on the spot's centuries-old charm. Part of the Hilliard Mills complex in Manchester, a nationally listed historic site, the brick building once housed a factory where George Washington's inaugural suit was made; later, it was used to produce uni-forms for Union soldiers. Now that we were on the premises, we couldn't wait to start making some Connecticut history of our own—until we realized that all of the Old World ambience we found so appealing came at an uncomfortably steep price: practicality. I am entirely willing to repeatedly admit throughout this book our naïveté in leaping headfirst into an old and complicated industry. My attempt to save face is in demonstrating what we learned from it.

The first, most obvious problem was that the space had no loading dock, which meant every time a tractor trailer showed up with a delivery of, say, 10,000 glass bottles, we had to unload everything by hand (oftentimes in the snow, rain, or mud) and lug it inside the building ourselves. Another essential feature that was missing from our Hilliard Street space, most unfortunately, was a bathroom. The nearest facility was all the way on the other side of the complex! Clearly, our minds clouded with enthusiasm, Pete and I had overlooked a few very important factors when we signed our lease. As a result, one of the first things we started planning, only a few months after getting set up at the Manchester site, was our eventual relocation to a bigger, better site—but it wasn't going to be easy. The Bureau of Alcohol, Tobacco, Tax, and Trade Bureau and Firearms regulates every drop of alcohol produced in this country so strictly that moving our entire base of operations would be more or less like starting from scratch, at least in terms of paperwork, permits, permissions, and approval.

Allow me to digress for just a moment on the complicated art of getting local and state approval for a liquor distillery. Between architectural plans, equipment purchases, local fire marshal and zoning approval, TTB (federal agency) approval, and state operating approval, opening a distillery can be a daunting task. Before our brand was well known in our area, moonshine wasn't an easy sell to local officials—even though it's no different than any other whiskey or vodka. It just sounded a bit too badass for our New England puritans to stomach easily, I guess! I found the easiest way to go about this was to start at the top. Mayors love touting new businesses opening up in their towns, as do town economic development teams. If you can "sell" your venture adequately to those in charge of attracting new business to their communities, you'll put a positive trickle-down effect in motion. You'll win higher-level champions who will help their enforcement teams understand the project better. Then, when it's time for approvals, you'll have a whole team of people helping rather than hindering you. There's nothing worse than having to deal with a code enforcement official coming in and making up an entire list of silly things they didn't tell you in the beginning so they can justify their jobs. Don't underestimate the value of time spent creating community champions for your project. The feds require everything you can imagine in the distilled spirits permit application, from background checks to a full security analysis of your site, even requiring the diagrams of the locks used on your doors. They also require full formula approval (recipe and process) and label approvals, which can take months to come in. The process of opening a distillery, we found, is not an easy one when compared to even a brewery or winery. And when you relocate, you have to do it all over again.

Anyway, back to the tale. For a period of months, Pete and I were preoccupied with the insatiable horizon known as "The New Building." As in, *Once we get to the new building, everything's going to be so much better. Once we get to the new building, all of our problems will be solved!* Fast-forward to the present: We've been in our new building in East Hartford for a couple years. Formerly used as the First National Bakery where Wonder Bread was made, it contains 400 acres of covered warehouse space; of that, we have about 12,000 square feet that we use for offices and production space. We have skylights, a loading dock— even bathrooms! Alas, it's still not quite enough. Our new insatiable horizon is finding a truly beautiful destination site, someplace with trees and a pond, a world-class setting fit to be the home of a world-class spirit. It's an insatiable horizon that will involve a fair amount of serendipity (not to mention synchronicity) to achieve, so for now, we're focusing on opening up a tasting room at the current site—another horizon that's required some aggressive obstacle crushing on our parts.

When we first moved into the East Hartford location, we weren't even allowed to consider a tasting room. At that time, Connecticut state liquor regulations allowed vineyards and breweries to have tasting rooms on site, but distilleries were forbidden to do the same. This was due to the fact that no one had asked to amend this law since the existence of prohibition. We were still dealing with blue law issues! (By the way, speaking of outdated laws, it's technically still illegal to cross a street in Hartford while walking on your hands. If you have the freedom to exercise this God-given right in your town, I strongly suggest you take advantage of it while you still can.) Still, Pete and I both firmly believe that an attractive, comfortable tasting room is exactly what Onyx customers deserve; in fact, we're constantly fielding queries from fans who want to come in, and see where and how their favorite spirit is produced. So what did we do? We lobbied to get the legislation changed— and it worked! On that note, I was new to hiring a lobbyist and didn't truly understand the process. We formed a trade group called the Connecticut

Small Brand Council, of which I am president, and involved local liquor retailers, producers, and distributors. By pooling our funds together, we were able to advocate, through the hiring of an experienced lobbyist, for sensible law changes at the capital and the introduction of laws that would benefit our industry locally. Since we've also introduced laws and protected laws that help our retailers, we've found our retail customer base appreciates us even more for helping them protect their businesses from the never-ending onslaught of new laws that will further regulate them to their detriment.

Now we're in the process of building a tasting room that will both add immeasurably to the experience of loyal Onyx drinkers who want to visit the grounds, as well as attract new customers. Will our drive to create and meet insatiable horizons end with the opening of our tasting room or the acquisition of an exquisite estate dedicated to all things Onyx? Of course not. We're human beings, and human beings are programmed to always want more. This impulse isn't necessarily a bad thing; the key is recognizing that insatiable horizons are there, and that if you don't guide them and keep them healthy, they'll end up guiding you.

If you aren't careful about choosing and chasing your own series of insatiable horizons, you'll most likely find yourself trapped on a hamster wheel, running after the vague fantasy of some stroke of luck that might relieve you of your weightiest responsibilities: *If I could just get that promotion, if I could just win the lotto, everything would be okay.* Not only is everything rarely "okay" when these things actually happen (if they ever do at all), this tunnel-vision thinking is the exact opposite of the kind of high-level vision you need to cultivate if you truly want to become a successful entrepreneur. Life is very much like sailing a little catboat in uncharted waters. People who don't have a clear vision of where they're headed are just sailing around in circles, going wherever the wind takes them, which means they often end up somewhere they never wanted to go in the first place. Sailors with a clear destination in mind, however, are much more likely to arrive at a place they're happy to be, even if they do get blown off course from time to time on the way. Another issue with insatiable horizons like winning the lotto is that this kind of thing is completely out of your control. Repeat after me: Goals should be limited to what you can control—what you can legitimately quantify and work toward achieving. Getting attached to the idea of attaining things that are outside the realm of your control (like a winning lotto ticket) means you're destined to either a life of disappointment or one that's rooted in pure luck. This is not to say that luck doesn't exist; personally, I think of luck as hard work meeting opportunity.

When creating your own insatiable horizon, look at precisely what your vision entails. Those insatiable horizons will change and evolve as you learn and grown, which is a very positive thing. For some people, this can take a lifetime. For others, it only takes a car ride. That's how it happened for my wife, Regina. Years before we were married, we were driving in the car on a weekend trip to Cape Cod. I'd recently failed out of college; Regina was on her way to graduating with honors—but she was the one having a meltdown over her future. Facing a mountain of student loan debt, Regina (a journalism/political science major) suddenly realized that she had no idea what she actually wanted to do with her life. "I just don't know what to do," she said, over and over again. "I have to get a job and pay off these loans, and I have no idea what to do." My hands firmly on the wheel, I told Regina to pull a notebook out of her bag. "From now on, this is going to be your goal notebook," I said. As the numbers on the odometer climbed, we talked about the kind of life Regina wanted to live and the kind of work she ultimately felt best suited to perform. We talked about her interests, her passions. We talked about her fears and hopes. By the time we got to Cape Cod, Regina decided she wanted to go to law school. We thought through some long-term goals and short-term execution lists. There were inevitably changes, but overall, she crafted a picture that guided her to right to the success she envisioned. She's since become a successful attorney who's published two books on controversial court cases in Connecticut. Her other passion is wine, and as a way to ensure a healthy connection to her other interests, she's started a highly successful wine review blog, WineEsquire .com. All the while, she stayed true to the practice of jotting down her goals—guiding her insatiable horizons—in her trusty notebook.

There's a lot to be said for being able to map out an entire life in the span of a three-hour car ride. The magic Regina and I managed to tap into on that trip is twofold. First of all, I firmly believe that travel—even a day trip to the shore—is a great and powerful way to get the ball rolling when you have some major life decisions to make. Consider the symbolism: thinking about the future while literally *moving forward.* That's why I tell entrepreneurs who are struggling to figure out what their next step should be to get in a car and drive. Drive, dream, figure it out—then come home and make that dream a reality.

Next, there's the even more powerful mojo associated with the physical action of writing down those dreams. Keeping a goal notebook and putting pen to paper on a daily basis is the best way I know to alter the plot of your always-evolving personal narrative. By writing down your goals religiously, you're literally writing your life story. And when you do, remember that goals should always be written in the present tense: *I am a successful moonshiner,* as opposed to *I will be a successful moonshiner.* Brian Tracy, best-selling author and entrepreneur, taught me this particular trick.

Of course, simply keeping a notebook isn't enough. After you set your goals, you have to take corresponding actions to help you reach them. It's been said that the average person makes approximately 35,000 tiny decisions every day. If you start every day by writing down your goals, I guarantee you that those goals are going to have a psychological impact on every tiny decision you make—and as time goes by, you're inevitably going to find yourself closer to your goals. Decisions translate to actions. What actions can you take, every day, to bring you closer to your goals—no matter how tired and beat down you are? How can you roll your sleeves up and get the job done? There are steps you can take every single day to keep you on your chosen path, and if you dedicate yourself to the practice of writing down your dreams on a daily basis, you're working toward your goals in ways you don't even realize.

But let's say, like Regina at the beginning of our trip, you're still stuck on defining your insatiable horizons. You have to figure out where you want to go before you can even start to think about how to get there, right? Interestingly enough, planning a future isn't all that different from planning a vacation. The first thing you want to do is think about what you like to do—or in other words, take stock of your strengths and weaknesses. Maybe you're a people person, and it's the idea of helping others that gets you out of bed every morning. Maybe you're never more alive than when you're brainstorming solutions to everyday problems, when you're coming up with new and inventive products or ways to make the world a better place. Whatever your strengths and weaknesses might be, play to them. Imagine, envision, and dream of a world you would be happy to inhabit. At the same time, ask yourself: What is happiness? For that matter, what is success? What does success really represent? In the traditional sense, being a successful entrepreneur means that your venture has brought you some degree of financial wealth. Personally, I believe that the concept of wealth goes beyond what's in your bank account. Wealth, to me, is better described as financial freedom because financial freedom, ultimately, translates to just plain freedom in general. Having financial freedom means you don't have to worry as much about things like paying bills, which in turn leaves you emotionally free to focus on creating a better world. In a better world, you prosper further; the cycle repeats itself with the added benefit of scaling up. And perhaps most important, having wealth means being in the position to give back to your community.

That last part—the question of creating a better world—was one of the last pieces of the puzzle to fall into place for me with Onyx. Although I was truly inspired by the idea of rebooting a centuries-old, homegrown industry, it took me a while to really come to terms with how opening a moonshine distillery would fulfill the criteria of "giving back" to my community. Aside from the fact that we were creating jobs and helping to stimulate the local economy, we were essentially just giving people one more reason to party. This isn't such a bad thing, but still, I wasn't quite at peace in my heart with the question of how our business would truly make a positive difference in the world. The answer, believe it or not, came in a Facebook post. Being huge believers in the power of promotion via social media, Pete and I have worked hard from the first days of Onyx to build a strong, vibrant Facebook community—and one of the best ways to do that is by starting meaningful, engaging conversations. To that end, I'd posted something along the lines of "Share the very first experience you had with Onyx moonshine." The response was instantaneous and overwhelming: Customers couldn't wait to share their stories, and nearly all of them were either hilarious or heartwarming, sometimes both. One comment, however, really stood out. It was from a woman who had recently lost her sister to cancer. Just two weeks prior to her sister's death, she wrote, the two sisters sat down with a bottle of Onyx by a campfire and "talked and laughed and cried all night long." "It's the last memory I have of her," the woman wrote, "and the first time in months that we were able to share a moment like that."

That's when I finally understood our true purpose as moonshiners. When enjoyed responsibly, Onyx moonshine is an excuse to sit down with somebody you love, put the technology away for a little while, and create a memory. Asking ourselves "What is Onyx moonshine?" began to provoke a different answer from us. Yes, it's a premium moonshine, but diving deeper helped us to answer what the product should really mean for consumers. So many of us make purchases not based on what something technically is, but what it represents to us. Emotion-based decision-making is absolutely something we're all guilty of. Think of any brands you're truly loyal to, the kind of car you wish you could have, or your favorite sports teams. Do you like them because each one of them

is without a doubt superior to any competing product? Of course not. You have memories, an emotional experience, and something you relate to that
happily allows you to stand behind the banner flag
of that product as yours. This is especially true in
the spirits business, where traditionally consumers
are much less likely to jump around to all different brands and categories—as you often see with
wine and beer. Spirits consumers tend to like one
or two brands that are their go-to because of what
that brand represents to them. Whether it's aspira-
tional or something their dad drank all those years
ago, there is an emotional connection to it that sur-
passes logic. As you look to develop your business,
look hard at what your brand will represent to customers in a true, emotional way. You may discover
a mission statement that gives your venture even
more momentum. To us, Onyx moonshine can be
the catalyst for the creation of special moments for
people to share, slow down, and enjoy some life.
Recognizing the potential purpose and meaning behind our product only served to amplify
our drive as entrepreneurs and businesspeople: to
create, and through our creation make life better
for people. That goes back to something I learned

back during my days at Xavier: the importance of a commitment to serving others. I always say, to truly understand what it's like to become an entrepreneur, go wait tables at a restaurant. If you really want to learn how to put your ego aside and make other people happy, there's no better way than by literally serving others. And the endless pursuit of serving others well is an insatiable horizon that will serve *you* well throughout your entire career.

Apple Hot Toddy

2 oz. Onyx Moonshine Apple Honey

3 oz. hot water

1/2 tsp local honey

Orange wedge for garnish

For centuries, whiskey has been used as a home remedy to fight myriad illnesses from common colds to toothaches. This modern twist on the hot toddy uses Onyx Apple Honey, made with hand-picked Connecticut honeycrisp apples. Tastes like a dream and doesn't require an illness to enjoy!

CHAPTER 5

TRILLIONS OF DOLLARS IN THE AIR

Tapping Into the Abundance All Around You

As I mentioned, I'm descended on my mother's side from the Chafee family, a pioneering New England clan that settled in Rhode Island and Connecticut back in the day when being a New Englander meant more than driving a Volvo. In the early 1900s, my great-grandfather, Jarius Charles Chafee, owned Chafee's Hotel in Middletown, Connecticut. During prohibition, when Chaffee's Hotel regularly accommodated a steady stream of visitors, and the speakeasy in the basement regularly accepted a steady stream of moonshine delivered via a small steamship we had on the Connecticut River, a sign hung on the stone fireplace with our family motto: "As we journey through life, let us live by the way."

A line from the traditional Scottish broadside ballad "We've Aye Been Provided For," the full stanza reads:

Let the miser delight in the hoarding of pelf,
For he has not the soul to enjoy it himself;
Since the bounty of Providence is new every day,
As we journey through life let us live by the way.

What does it mean—and what is pelf?! Pelf is money, and the meaning of the lyric, as I understand it, is that the single-minded pursuit of money is bound to bring misery—whereas trusting in the abundant nature of the Universe and making the decision to be fully present in every moment will naturally lead to health, wealth, and happiness. If you, like so many people, feel like "trusting in the abundant nature of the universe" is a bit of a gamble, consider this: The vast majority of financial transactions nowadays happen in the digital sphere, which means that at any given moment, there are billions of "dollars" being transmitted from one satellite to the next. To put it more bluntly, at any given moment there are virtually trillions of dollars *floating through the air*. Binary money molecules are flowing through my glass of Onyx at this very moment! Imagine yourself inside one of those money booths they have on game shows where contestants step inside and paw wildly at the air as dollars are blown around their heads. Whether or not you realize it, you're standing (or sitting) inside one of those money booths at all times. It's just a matter of figuring out the right strategy for grabbing the money you need, when you need it. Picturing yourself inside a money booth is the perfect meditation when you begin the important work of raising money for your project. If you've not raised money before, this is a great mantra to begin the process. The money is everywhere, and people don't have enough places to put it or enough smart entrepreneurs to give it to. Before you can even think about approaching investors, you'll need to have a stellar business plan in place. A daunting task, to be sure, but there are luckily tons of great resources for help in writing a business plan, from books to articles to online templates. In most states and communities, there are also organizations like SCORE, the SBA, and others that offer free help to get you on your way to planning your business. Of course, nothing beats having a mentor or friend in your network who's done it before and can coach you through the process. Hell, you can even call me! (I do charge, of course. *Wink.*) The truth is, there's no real steadfast rule for how a business plan should be written. Both the process and end result really depend on the specifics of your project. A business plan done internally, for your eyes only, might cut to the chase and be more direct than one offered to investors, which might need to include more evidence of support on the validity of your business model. When creating any plan, the key is to focus on the good old-fashioned *W*s: who, what, where, why, and when. In other words, who are you selling to and why are they your customer? What are you selling to them, and why is this necessary in the market? Where will you be producing the product, or where will you be providing the service? Where are your customers located, and how will you get it to your customers in that market? Why is this product or service important, and how will it generate cash flow for the business? Finally, when will you begin selling the actual product, need more funding, and/or sell the company? (These last points are meant to answer the foremost question on every investor's mind: *When can you pay me back my money!*)

Another thing to consider is whether or not there's any substantial research and development (R&D) or lead time before you're ready to go to market. As I mentioned earlier, setting up a distillery and getting approvals take a long time. You need to have a location and to pay rent before you're approved to sell product! You can't even distill spirits at home without a distilled spirits permit—so R&D is impossible without everything in place. One challenge for us has also been forecasting the lead time for our Secret Stash Whiskey because the production involves aging—unlike with moonshine that pours right from the still into a bottle or your mouth. That's why some new distilleries operate like vineyards, waiting years before they release their first product. This ties up capital for a long time. Both you and your investors will want to get a good idea of the reality of your business plan. Stay concise in your planning, do your research, know your competitors inside and out, know your customers like family, and know your product better than the back of your hand. Avoid getting too sales-pitchy in tone while writing the business plan; this isn't *Shark Tank*. This business plan is your road map. Present the strong facts as they are. If your plan is clear and well thought out, the success potential will be clear to both you and your investors. The proof will be in the pudding, or, in our case, in the moonshine.

Let's assume now that your business plan is done and that you understand the full scope of your project and what it will cost. You've spoken to a variety of people in your chosen industry and put together an informal board of advisors who can guide you through the process of raising funds. Let's also assume that you have absolutely no money of your own. That's how it was for me when I first started out in the business world, after all: I'd failed out of college and was roughly $30,000 in debt; my mother had put my things in the condo parking lot and moved away. Had my grandmother not graciously allowed me to sleep on her couch, I would have most likely ended up crashing at the YMCA in Hartford (only $8 per night, but no crossing the streets on your hands).

This might sound like a set of particularly extreme circumstances, but the truth is, many entrepreneurs find themselves in similar situations when they're starting out. In fact, these dire circumstances are often what drives people to go into business in the first place! Having no money of your own isn't as much of an obstacle as you might think. This lack of personal funds simply means that you'll need to master the art of gaining access to what is called OPM (other people's money).

The first and most critical lesson to learn when it comes to raising OPM is this somewhat counter-intuitive truth that was said to me once by a friend and highly successful venture capital firm founder: *If you ask someone for money, you'll get advice; if you ask someone for advice, you'll get money.*

Part of the reason why this works could be considered Dale Carnegie 101: Everyone—successful businesspeople, investors, and entrepreneurs included—responds to feeling like someone is genuinely interested in their lives. That's why the CEO of the food distribution company I talked about in Chapter 2 had such a generous reaction (generous to the tune of $150,000) when I expressed an interest in the nuts and bolts of his business. I was genuinely curious about how his company worked, and that made him feel good. It reminded him that he was, indeed, a success, and that he was in a position to pass on the secrets and resources of that success to the next generation. Considering how well the strategy of expressing genuine interest and showing true respect for an established business-person worked for us, you can see why I'm a firm believer in the "ask for advice" principle. However, that experience leads us to another, equally critical, bullet point that was also stated by said VC friend: *Not all money is green.* The CEO of the food distribution company was a good investor for us on many levels, and someone I'll appreciate until the end of my days, but he was ultimately not the right kind of investor for our project. An established businessman, he nevertheless knew next to nothing about the costs and effort associated with creating a spirit brand because he'd purchased his company from his father when it was already up and running (and turning a profit). Consequently, everything he knew about making money related to maintaining profitability, rather than the initial process of accumulating capital and market share. Because we were also new to this game, we drastically underestimated our startup costs—which in turn meant that if we followed our hearts and made moonshine (as opposed to a vodka or limoncello like our investor expected) it would take longer than he'd originally hoped for him to make his money back. Currently, having realized that his vision and our vision are radically different, we're working to buy him out. But we could have saved ourselves a considerable amount of hassle and headaches if we'd been more conscious of what to look for in an investor right from the beginning. That's why I recommend interviewing investors in the same way they're going to interview you.

First, you want to learn everything you can about what kind of people they are. In our business, it's easy to get to know a potential investor: We take them out to one of our customer restaurants, sit down, and drink moonshine. I'm a big proponent of getting out from behind your desk and going somewhere with anyone you might add to your team or bring on as an investor. Have them over to your house for dinner or for brunch on a Sunday. Relate to them on a personal level.

Second, you'll want to know if they're familiar in your space. That's why one of my first questions for would-be financiers is if they've ever worked or invested in the beverage industry, or, at the very least, in consumer goods or brand building. It's always a big plus if your investors have contacts to share or even intellectual capital they can bring to the table along with their funds. Now, it's not necessarily a deal breaker if they aren't experienced in your trade—but you'll find communication will be easier if they are. At the same time, if they've been in your industry for their entire lives, they may be so entrenched in how things are done that they won't be able to see the value of the opportunities your venture would create (like all of those "experts" who told us we should make vodka instead of moonshine).

Next, you'll want to find out if investors are flush enough to regularly participate in new projects. No matter how much someone loves your idea, trust me: If they can't afford to lose the money they're investing in you, it's not going to be an enjoyable ride for you or them. I heard a friend whose job was to raise money for new ventures say once to an investor, "If I lose this check on the way to the bank, is it going to ruin your life?" If the answer is an honest yes, do not accept that money.

For you to be successful in the long run, it's critical that you maintain an honest, reliable reputation. If your investor doesn't truly understand the risk associated with your venture, then you're not being a responsible entrepreneur, and someday you'll end up stuck with an unethical reputation. If they've invested in other projects, don't be afraid to ask to speak with those investees (I actually don't know if that's even a word, but it is now!). You need to have a firm grasp on their expectations. We turned one deal down because the small group of investors wanted us to decrease our salaries, which certainly weren't anything huge to begin with. (This was after taking exceptionally small payments the first two years we were open.) Their request served as a warning sign on two levels: (1) They were clearly unsophisticated (inexperienced and underfunded) because if they were more savvy, they would have known that you can't have your entrepreneurs hurting for cash and expect them to perform well for you; and (2) if they felt we should keep the capital for other reasons, then it meant they believed we were probably undercapitalized and were prepping to take advantage of us at a later phase of fundraising.

It's very important to find out if investors will be the types to sit back silently and let you do your thing without getting involved, or if they'll expect to be afforded a certain degree of influence over your company's vision, or even a hands-on role in the day-to-day decision making process. Swim these waters very, very carefully. Do you want an investor or a partner? These can be very different things. Investors should let you run the show because they believe in you and your plan, and I don't say that lightly. They're investing because they believe—in order of importance—in *you* and in your plan. That said, if you're at a point where big money people (we're talking venture capitalists) want in on your success, you might need to consider them as partners. They may even be able to help you see that you've led the company to this point, but to truly succeed a CEO will need to be put in place. And that might be the best thing for you and the business. Think hard about your long-term strategy here; it will affect your lifestyle and future.

When vetting your investors, Google the hell out of them. Read about past deals they've done, and investigate any lawsuits (if that applies!). Read anything you can find to understand everything they've done. If they're entirely MIA from your internet sources, well, it's 2015, and that's a weird sign.

Eventually, a terms sheet and operating agreement will be presented, and that's really where all the nitty-gritty details come to light. Your operating agreement is the Magna Charta of your business. Legally binding, it's the agreement set forth among you, partners, and potential investors. It's the law that structures and governs your business. As such, you must be clear and up-front from the beginning. If you verbally agree to one thing in the operating agreement you submit and fail to stick to it, you can bet that's going to freak people out. And don't be cheap and skip out on a lawyer or hire the guy who drives around in a 1986 Lincoln handing out his magnets around town. Get an attorney that knows business deals. You can marry one like I did, which saves money (this is arguable), or hire one you feel comfortable with.

At the end of the day, we gave away equity in our company for $150,000 of much-needed capital. Our inaugural investor had access to this capital, which is why I approached him. As I said, ultimately he was not the right kind of investor for our project, but there were things about him at the time that were right for us—namely, the fact that he was an "angel investor." What is an angel investor? Before we get into the definition, let's start by talking a bit about the different types of investors and funding sources you'll learn about during your initial capital-raising phase, and the pros and cons of each.

1. Friends and Family

Pros: The most informal option when it comes to soliciting startup money, friends and family will most likely be far less demanding than banks or venture capitalists when it comes to cashing in on their investment. This is most likely the most "patient" form of startup capital.

Cons: Even if they're not expecting to make a huge profit on their investment, money from friends and family generally comes with strings of some kind attached. So if you're not prepared for years of unsolicited advice from Aunt Edith on how best to run your business or reminders every Christmas from your grandmother about all that money she lent you when you were starting out, you might want to consider blood relatives and close acquaintances as a last resort when it comes to fundraising. Naturally, this all depends on the resources individuals have access to, as well as the nature of your specific relationships.

2. Angel Investors

Pros: Usually wealthy individuals with an income of at least $200,000 per year and/or a net worth of $1 million, angel investors are eager to invest in start-ups (typical investments run between $25,000 and $1.5 million) because they're hoping for a higher rate of return than they would get investing in the stock or real estate market. Signing up an angel investor generally results in a lump-sum payment, and the process is often fairly quick.

Cons: Angel investors are generally somewhat hesitant when it comes to follow-up investments, want a high rate of return (usually 25% or more), and may expect some control over your company (even though they may or may not have expertise in your given industry). I've found these guys can often think themselves a bit more sophisticated than they really are and occasionally can overcomplicate things for relatively small investments.

3. Venture Capitalists

Pros: Venture capital firms work much the same way as angel investors, except they have more access to funds (average investments run between $500,000 and $5 million); this is also all these guys do, so most VC firms also offer access to expert consultants in your field and might serve as connections to other potential (and potentially heavy-hitting) investors.

Cons: Venture capitalists typically expect an even higher rate of return on their investments than angel investors (50% or more), as well as equity and a greater degree of control. They also tend to take longer than angel investors to make a decision. These types of investors are intelligent, are highly sophisticated, and can quickly extrapolate truths from your numbers, projections, and plans that you might not have even realized existed. I recommend having an equally sophisticated advisor/friend/mentor who can help you navigate these occasionally shark-infested waters, lest you accidentally find yourself out of necessity founding a venture that improves prosthetic limbs!

Unless you're independently wealthy, it's unlikely that you'll be able to get a business off the ground without utilizing one or more types of investors listed above, and it's important that you don't feel limited to traditional means of money raising—especially today, in the era of crowdfunding. Kickstarter and GoFundMe are great examples of platforms that will help you to access capital without being forced to give away equity in your company or even offer returns on investments (apart from some type of "reward," which can be as expensive or inexpensive as you want it to be).

These latest advances in fundraising also make it easier for entrepreneurs to avoid the soulcrushing process of applying for bank loans, which may be impossible to secure anyway, if you don't have a ton of assets. Think of it like this: Banks will give you money for collateral, period—unless you have a very strong, steady cash flow they can prove won't be going anywhere. (That's a "problem" when you don't actually own much of anything, like me. I put just about everything I can in my wife's name, apart from the shares I own in our ventures, which don't always seem to be worth a whole lot on paper!) This touches on a topic for a whole different book, but the message is: You never want to be wealthy on paper if you can avoid it.

Hopefully, you'll be in a position soon where this is by choice!

Banks also have pretty aggressive loan rates that can tie up your cash flow until you've paid them off completely. Plus, banks are in the business of lending out *your* money from your checking and savings account, then lending it back to you so you can buy your house and start your business. (That said, it's not a bad idea to keep the bank option open if possible, perhaps by maintaining a relationship with a banker who really knows his or her stuff.)

For us, tapping into federal and state government resources turned out to be a much wiser choice than signing our futures over to a bank would have been. Shortly after we launched Onyx for $150,000, we realized that we didn't have nearly enough money to keep up with our rapidly growing business—but the State of Connecticut did. After doing some investigation online, I found out that the Connecticut State Department of Economic and Community Development has a program that offers grant money and very low-interest-rate loans to local startup businesses. And after completing the (somewhat extensive) application process, we received a grant and a low-interest loan, partially forgivable, low-interest loan. Not only did these government funds make it possible for us to truly build a solid enterprise in those early days, the relationship we now have with the State of Connecticut continues to work in our favor. Because they recognize that our business drives the economy, the state has always been willing to do whatever they can to help us succeed. As a result, I believe that entrepreneurs would be foolish not to follow our lead and explore everything the federal and state government has to offer. Sure, accessing government funds is a somewhat complicated process—get ready for some major paperwork—but if you really want that money and don't want to sell your soul to the wrong investors, you're going to roll up your sleeves and get the work done.

Of course, for most entrepreneurs, the hard work of fundraising unfortunately doesn't end with that first round. As your business expands, you'll need more and more capital to keep it going—and in the first few years of your business, your profits likely won't cover the cost of expansion. Even if you are profitable, it's unlikely that the reinvestment of those profits will allow you to take advantage of the growth opportunities present to you. Bear in mind that most businesses aren't even profitable for the first three or four years. The concept of scalability, or the ability to accommodate growth, is crucial here. Entrepreneurs need adequate funds to accommodate the growth of their business. Assuming you want your business to grow, the last thing you want when starting out is to be undercapitalized—and Pete and I most certainly were. Sure, $150,000 dollars sounded like a lot of money considering our venture was purely a concept and relatively risky, but that was before we understood all the costs associated with manufacturing. We didn't expect Onyx to grow as quickly as it did—neither did our investor—so we underestimated how much money we would need for everything from supplies to staff. That's when those funds from the State of Connecticut really came in handy!

When you're looking to start a business, most experts will tell you to put a lot of time and effort into your financial projections. Projections are estimates of the future financial performance of your business, and as such, ideally should help you to map out your milestones, end goals and plan for potential variables, like the aforementioned issue of unexpectedly rapid growth. Realistically, however, projections are often highly inaccurate estimations rooted in either inexperience, an overly heady sense of optimism, or both. This is particularly true for start-ups like us. Having no experience with spirits production, when it came to numbers we were essentially just guesstimating. I was concerned about the possibility of our projections being unrealistic from the beginning, so one thing I did to try to build a real-life frame of reference was to research the workings of another super tiny boutique farm distillery in Connecticut. First, I went on their Website to find out how many stores carried their product. There were 80 stores listed. Next, I looked at those stores to get a sense of how much of the distillery's product they were selling, and decided each one must be selling roughly a case per month. Based on those findings, I figured these stores would sell about a case of Onyx per month, too. Within a week of launching, we exceeded those projections. So you want to make sure that your projections are realistic, but also positive—even aggressive. It's better to be prepared for growth than caught off guard and ill equipped when business booms.

At the same time, you don't want to be overcapitalized, either—for the simple reason that no matter what, you will make mistakes during the early years of your business, and if you're overcapitalized, you're doomed to lose more money making them (more on those mistakes in the next chapter). I've seen many breweries and distilleries start their businesses with the same level of experience Pete and I had when we started Onyx, only a lot more capital (think Wall Street folks who suddenly said, "Hey, I can make liquor!"). They made the same mistakes we did, but theirs were a lot more costly. This is why staging multiple capital raises in your plan can be very important, and should be tied directly to the milestones and goals you set before the next phase of funds is raised or released into your working capital account. Ask yourself seriously: Do you really need $1 million for your venture right now, or can you start with $250,000 and raise the next part once you've reached X in sales?

Ultimately, the question of how much capital you start out with is one of what kind of entrepreneur you are. Are you a micromanager by nature? Do you need to be involved in every detail of production? Do you see yourself as a long-term business manager? If your business is your baby and you can't imagine ever handing it over to someone else, you should know that venture capital firms may require you to bring in more highly skilled professionals to do your job after the venture is rolling. Remember: Venture capitalists want a hefty return, as quickly as possible, so they want your business to grow as quickly as possible—and if that means hiring someone more qualified than you to make that happen, well, so be it. You might even end up having to sell your business to meet their requirements. So if you're not comfortable thinking about an eventual exit strategy for your venture, you might not want to start out by approaching sophisticated investors (defined as having a net worth of at least $1 million).

Or maybe you're more of a visionary type, someone with a passion for creating who doesn't mind delegating day-to-day duties. Pete and I are both driven by the need to create, and keep creating. Whether it's a variation of one of our existing products or the building from scratch of an entirely new offering, we get high on the process of bringing something to life that previously didn't exist. Personally, I can't see myself in the same role, doing the same job, for 20 years. I identify more closely with Richard Branson (a visionary) than with Steve Jobs (a micromanager).

No matter what type of entrepreneur you are, remember that you can and will find the funds to make your project happen. Just think about that money booth! It might take months longer than you expect it to, and you may have to revise your business plans more times than you ever thought possible, but if you're willing to do the work, the money will come, and it's waiting for you to grab it and put it to work!

New England Sling

2 oz. Secret Stash Reserve Whiskey
1/2 oz. cherry liqueur or cherry juice
1/2 Tbs. simple syrup
1 oz. fresh lemon juice
dash of fruit bitters

Shake ingredients over ice. Strain and garnish with a twist of lemon or a cherry.

Slings were made for over a century before the term "cocktail" was coined. Traditionally made with fruit, bitters, and a bit of fizzy water, this New England Sling gets its authentic flavor from Connecticut's first whiskey, Secret Stash.

CHAPTER 6

Rock Bottom to Bottoms Up

Why Falling Behind Is Key to Moving Forward

Failure rocks. In my opinion, the F-word can be a more valuable learning tool than success, so embrace it. For one thing, there's nothing like failure to challenge your growth as an entrepreneur. For another, facing failure definitely seems to have a way of revealing someone's true character. One thing's for certain: Your plan never goes exactly how you originally intended—and sometimes (often) these unexpected glitches involve varying degrees of failure. The question to ask is this: When things fall apart, are you one to stand right back up and make alterations to your plan as needed, or do you give up and settle for less than you deserve? Like Winston Churchill said, "Success consists of going from failure to failure without loss of enthusiasm." If there's one thing every single successful businessperson I've met has in common, it's that they've all failed at one point, if not several points—sometimes monumentally! Part of what makes business such a fantastic adventure is how adaptable you can learn to become, because being an entrepreneur is one of the ultimate means for personal expression, creation, and human development. Investors we work with and those on our team know this about us for certain: We never, ever give up. Those around us know that and believe no challenge or failure will keep us down, and this means an absolute success in the long run.

As I mentioned in Chapter 1, Pete and I had one of our first major failures with THAZOO.com—an idea that was strikingly similar to Facebook, years before Facebook launched. As young and inexperienced as we were, we didn't realize the potential impact of our idea; consequently, we were too blind to hire people more qualified than we were to help bring that idea to life. God, I can't emphasize enough how much I loathe the old mentality that it's cheaper for us to do the work ourselves. If this is you, let me save you a couple years and a lot of stress. Budget your venture to build a top-notch team from day one and don't accept anything else. Pete and I didn't know enough about computer coding, for one thing, to build a successful social media platform; we also didn't know how to monetize what we wanted to build. By the way, this is actually a more common theme in today's tech world than we realized. From an objective standpoint, THAZOO.com was an outright failure. (You're welcome, Zuckerberg.) We didn't have the insight, wisdom, or team behind us to know what we were really doing. At the same time, through that experience, Pete and I learned how to throw amazing events, a skill we often put to use for Onyx. It's always worth analyzing your failures, taking what you can from those disappointments, and applying the lessons you learned to your next project. We make it a point to never complain, and we absolutely never, ever place the blame on anyone else but us—even if there were others involved who may have contributed to a particular failure. We are all where we are at this exact moment as a result of a million tiny decisions we've made that led us to exactly this place, good or bad or both. This "absolute responsibility" gives us a sense of responsibility and control over our environment, and anything outside of that control isn't worth stressing a single second about.

Of course, not all lessons translate from one project to the next, and conscious learning from new experiences should be a lifelong mission that will never get boring. Every venture you could ever dream up will come with its own built-in opportunities for new and exciting ways to screw up. By the time Pete and I were in the process of getting Onyx off the ground, thanks to all of the lessons we had learned in our other ventures, we felt we had built up a good mental toolkit of all the principles and knowledge we'd need to employ to make a viable that will succeed. We still knew nothing about the day-to-day reality of running a distillery, or any form of manufacturing for that matter. Initially, we knew there was a lot we didn't know, and in the beginning we didn't surround ourselves with people who had more knowledge specific to spirits production. Not only did we start off drastically undercapitalized (a mistake that has haunted us at many subsequent forks in the road as we've grown and developed), we also underestimated how much we would need to produce—as well as the supplies and, yes, capital we'd need to keep that unexpectedly higher volume of production going while still expanding distribution. We discovered a pretty complex formula that we must continually tweak as the business grows. As a result, we struggled for months to meet the demands of customers and retailers, which was not only extremely frustrating to our clients but detrimental to our business in a variety of ways. For example, because bars and restaurants couldn't reliably predict when they'd get their next delivery of Onyx, they couldn't give us cocktail menu placement, a critical piece of the marketing puzzle when releasing a new spirit into the market. This was completely understandable on their parts. No bar or restaurant owner wants to be put in the uncomfortable, unprofessional position of having to tell a thirsty customer, "Sorry, we're out of that right now." Still, it was particularly aggravating that our moonshine, which mixes so superbly, couldn't be included in our client's regular cocktail recipes. That's why entrepreneurs, particularly those selling an original product, need to absolutely make sure that their location and setup are in alignment with what the market is going to demand. Otherwise, if your rate of growth is faster than anticipated, you're going to end up sacrificing consistency or, equally as bad, overpromising and underdelivering to your customers. This is the challenging moment when your success actually causes damage to your business. It's ironic, but it happens often and it happened to us. During the business planning stage, you want to think through a variety of different possible outcomes, ranging from wild success to utter failure. If you're successful beyond your projections (the ideal situation, of course) what are the negative impacts this could have on the business? Are there potential supply issues or cash-flow issues due to your increased production? What about the outlaying of capital for supplies and the delay on your getting paid? If the launch is an utter failure, why might that occur? And what quick, strategic changes can you make to correct before you run out of time/ money and the whole thing goes bust? The military calls this model a "reverse planning sequence": They operate from the perspective that anything can be done; the question is how. This mission-oriented approach forces you to work backward and analyze different paths to take that will allow you to arrive at the same intended goal. If you have some contingency plans now, then you won't have to scramble to make them when the inevitable surprises surface.

The fact that Onyx was missing on cocktail menus in those early days served as an irritating reminder of our shortsightedness, but at least bars and restaurants were stocking our product, and for that, we were thankful—because the most painful failure Pete and I experienced as professional moonshiners was when the very first bar we approached flat-out refused to carry Onyx at all.

Allow me to set the scene for you as I wipe a lone, salty tear from my cheek: After submerging ourselves as deeply as possible in the spirits business for a couple of years, making countless batches of booze and recipe variations, after losing God knows how many nights of sleep over how to raise enough money and obsessing over the details of label design and bottle choice and literally every other detail of moonshine production imaginable, Pete and I were finally—finally!—ready to introduce our creation to the world. We walked into a bar in Manchester, armed with an expertly labeled bottle of Onyx and a well-rehearsed spiel on the history of moonshine and why our locally produced, high-end version of the stuff belonged behind this particular bar. We were, I would say, more than a little optimistic. This was the moment we'd been waiting and working for, so our stomachs pretty much dropped through the floor when our pitch was met with a big fat no. *No?!* Even worse than the owner/bartender's callous denial of the support we'd so hoped for was the fact that he didn't have any real reason for shooting us down. "I just can't picture this stuff in my bar," he said, shrugging.

Pete and I went back to the distillery that night pretty devastated, having been met out the gate with a big failure. Not a great morale booster. There we were, having spent thousands of dollars and hundreds of hours trying to create something truly spectacular, something that consumers would be dying to get their hands on, and the first bartender we approached didn't even want to hear what we had to say! It was the biggest letdown imaginable, and I'll admit that I didn't exactly have the warmest feelings toward that bartender for a while. Bartenders can sometimes have an amusingly emperor-like attitude about their ability to order or not order a particular product. In my years I've run into more than one ego, and if you've worked in the service business, you know exactly what I'm talking about. Now, let's quickly go back to the first page of this chapter and reread the quote from Winston Churchill. In retrospect, his snub was one of the best things that could have happened to us at the time. Because once that initial sting of rejection faded (which took about 15 minutes and a glass of Onyx on the rocks to fortify our spirits), Pete and I became more motivated than ever to succeed. That same night, we got all fired up (more Onyx on the rocks) and created the official Onyx bartender's guide. Filled with facts, history, and authentic prohibition-era cocktail recipes, the bartender's guide was designed to engage and inspire mixologists—and in turn, educate consumers—to move past the tired old vodka and cranberries or gin and tonics they've been pouring and drinking for years. We talked about the things they cared about. We allowed them to be the expert to their customers, and we presented the guidebook on vintage paper, with an old-school feel to it. It felt extremely authentic and had a kind of illicit speakeasy, prohibition-era feel. As soon as we were done with the guide, we sent it out to area bars and restaurants, hoping to spark an interest in Onyx, to start a conversation—and it worked. Our bartender's guide elicited the opposite reaction of that initial bartender's jaded disinterest. People were curious about our product. They wanted to try it for themselves. They asked questions. We asked questions, too, and in the process, we learned that every customer has different needs, and that it's our job as entrepreneurs to help them see how our product fills those individual needs. Some bartenders, for example, need to feel like they just discovered the "next big thing." For them, we played up Onyx-specific buzzwords (*handmade, high-end, craft*) and talked about how our company was at the forefront of a craft spirits trend. Other bar managers are all about the bottom line. In those cases, we talked about how Onyx is a premium, top-shelf spirit that's cheaper than Grey Goose (and mixes better, too!). Their margins are higher on Onyx, but they can charge the same price—so Onyx makes them more money. Other customers, those with a commitment to American-made, homegrown products, were sold simply on the local premise. The point is, we got their minds and mouths open, and they loved it.

As you develop a product or service, one of the best exercises you can do for your business plan is to create a "features and benefits" model of your creation. As I just mentioned, features and benefits change based on the audience you're talking to, but the concept is the same: features of the product and how that feature benefits the customer. Here's an example of a couple of features and benefits we might provide to our distributor salesmen, so they can sell our product better to bartenders.

FEATURES	BENEFITS
Onyx is a handmade, craft brand.	Customers want craft brands and pay more for them.
Onyx costs less than premium vodka.	Restaurants make higher margins per drink on Onyx.
We do seasonal releases.	There's always something new.

It comes down to this: The best salespeople are good listeners. And once they learn what's really driving their customers, they're savvy and knowledgeable enough to play up the specific features and benefits of their product that will be most desirable to that particular buyer. When going into a sales situation, always ask yourself: What questions can I ask to try to get an understanding of exactly this person's goals and challenges, and how can I help them solve them? Repeat what they tell you back to them, and then explain some features of your product and how it will benefit them, tailoring those benefits to that buyer's problems and needs.

Our initial sales failure was an incredibly painful one, but we moved on quickly and the process improved us. About six months later, when every restaurant around the bar that rejected us was carrying Onyx proudly, they put in a big order and acted like nothing ever happened. And we were back at the table and happy to support them, even planning a special moonshine-pairing dinner. Never forget that many, many businesses fail. I've heard it said that the average multimillionaire has experienced at least three major business failures. The fact that there exists the potential for the failure of your business will never mean the failure of your career as an entrepreneur. You never want to let the fear of failure stop you from heeding the siren's call. I know so many people who've had million-dollar ideas but never did anything with them, either because they didn't get off their butts or because they were terrified of falling on their faces. They wasted an incredible opportunity to bring a valuable, positive idea to life. This is life, the one thing we have complete control over! Why would anyone want to spend more than one more day not doing exactly what they want? You have an obligation to your soul, to your life on this planet, to get out there and get it done before you die. So you can either craft a fun, vibrant life for yourself just by writing down your goals down every day and taking every action you can to reach them, or you can just sit in your cubicle and bring home your paycheck and just try to survive until you're dead. Every night I ask myself, "Did I live the best day I could?" If I die in my sleep, I want to die with a big fat smile knowing the answer is *yes.*

Now that I've gone on for a few pages about how failure is nothing to fear and how falling back is the key to moving forward, I'm going to tell you something else—something that may seem contradictory at first: Failure is not an option. Not in the ultimate sense, anyway. Yes, temporary failure is inescapable, but you can never allow yourself to consider giving up as an alternative to success. If your subconscious mind knows that you can always bail when things get rough, then you're more likely to throw in the towel the second you're forced out of your comfort zone. That's why when Spanish conquistador Hernán Cortés arrived on the shore of Mexico with the intention of conquering the Aztecs and taking all of their gold back to Spain, he commanded his fleet of ships burned. With no way out, his troop of roughly 600 men had no choice but to forge ahead. Were those men scared? Undoubtedly so. They were most likely terrified, but that drive to survive motivated them in a way the mere promise of gold never could have done. Because of his bold decision, Cortés became the first man to successfully conquer Mexico. And he wasn't the only historical leader to employ this all-or-nothing tactic. About a thousand years earlier, Alexander the Great burned his ships upon arrival in Persia; he too was victorious. Of course, if you burn your ships and then lose the battle, well, that's that. But we don't read about those folks in the history books, do we? Like the lottery slogan goes, "You can't win if you don't play." In some ways, I've always felt that my choice to drop out of college was a bit like burning the ships. Considering I have no trade skills and no education, who would ever hire me for a job? I'm essentially forced to succeed as an entrepreneur, and to be honest, I have no desire to do anything else, anyway. This is so much fun, it's not work! And I don't have the false insatiable horizon that once I'm able to retire I can begin enjoying life because I have nothing to retire from.

It all comes down to your level of commitment. Are you committed enough to your project to burn your boats at the outset, or do you have a canoe tied to a secret dock somewhere just in case? I can tell you that when you begin dealing with investors and raising capital for your project, it will be a big bonus if those investors believe you will make the project a success no matter what, because you're all in. Remind yourself every morning when you open your eyes: no turning back. After all, if there's no going back, the only direction left to go is forward. I'll admit, it's easier to adopt this strategy when there's absolutely no way you can go back to whatever you were doing before. It's also easier to have a much higher risk tolerance when you're young and naïve. When I came home from college having flunked the majority of my classes, I was beyond distraught. I felt like I'd let my entire family down (they felt the same way), wasted thousands of dollars in tuition, and effectively burned any and all bridges to a higher education or a well-paying job. The only path left for me was that of becoming a self-made man. Once I recognized and accepted this truth, I ran down that path at breakneck speed and haven't looked back since. This is another great example of having a monstrous failure and taking full advantage of it, allowing failure to awaken another voice within, learning from that failure, and having it blossom into something special that might not have come otherwise. As I look back now, had I succeeded at school and gotten a great job, I might be heading into my office cubicle right now, making someone else's dream a reality, while the make-believe allure of job stability keeping me from fulfilling my inner calling. It's like a nightmare!

As you consider your own ability to create something that would be incredibly successful and profitable for you, focus on completing the process of vetting your idea. Through conversation, research, and hard work, you'll arrive at a place where you can either proceed or not. Let your list of goals and subsequent decisions do all the work for you, while you simply take action. Once you feel you've got something incredible by the tail, grab it and don't let go! Some things may not work; others will. But giving up is not an option, and never giving it a go is even worse!

Rattlesnake Bite

1 1/2 oz. Onyx Moonshine
1 Tbsp maple syrup or liqueur
Juice of 1/2 a lime
1 bottle of your favorite local dark beer (porters work well)
Dash of cayenne powder

Add ingredients to a pint glass with ice. Stir to combine.

This sweet and spicy beer cocktail combines powerful flavors that hang in a delicate balance. Kick up the cayenne for a sensational drinking experience.

CHAPTER 7

ANYTHING THEY CAN DO, YOU CAN DO BETTER

Turning Mediocre Markets Into Goldmines

As the saying goes, there's nothing new under the sun. This universal truth presents something of a challenge to aspiring entrepreneurs, who are in the unique position of having to convince the world at large that their product or service is best of its kind—even when there are countless other variations on that product or service available to consumers. That's why the smartest startup businesses find a way to identify and solve problems in the market that some other company hasn't already solved, or they fill a need that hasn't already been filled. A tall order, to be sure, but this doesn't mean you have to reinvent the wheel. In fact, some of the most famously successful projects are those that put a slight tweak on an already-indispensable product.

Facebook is a perfect example of an inevitable product (or service, depending on how you look at it). Obviously, Pete and I knew that when we launched THAZOO.com, we didn't execute it properly—and now Facebook is worth tens of billions of dollars. But Facebook was far from the last inevitable venture, and there will be more and more forever. Humans are on the verge of commercializing space, opening up infinite new opportunities for business ventures that will push our limits to the stars—and make some people extraordinarily wealthy in the process. As an entrepreneur, it is challenging to not have ideas every day that could be worth pursuing. This is something I struggle with often because focus is also very necessary for success. Just yesterday, I was in rush hour in my car, thinking about solar panels and wondering when somebody's going to figure out how to flake solar panel chips into car paint jobs for free power. You may have an idea that is complex, or it could be shockingly simple: a better coffee cup or a way to make changing baby diapers a less gruesome chore, a small but significant twist that makes something people use every day more efficient, or more fun, or safer. We're simply making a moonshine we can legally sell, we haven't truly done anything that hasn't been done for hundreds of years a million times before in America. Our "twist" is the quality, and the fact that it's legal! Very often, people are faced with a brilliant idea right under their nose that they simply haven't noticed. I have a friend who has decided to change her career path from studying for her law degree to becoming a court reporter (you know, the people who spend all their time in the courtroom type, type, typing away in some weird character shorthand on those crazy old typewriters). Seems like a fine enough choice of career, but to me, the inevitability of that job going extinct due to changes in technology seems to be looming on a not-too-distant horizon. I would think those two years devoted to learning how to become a human typewriter would perhaps have been better spent designing the inevitable solution—which would certainly conclude with a better payout! If you're searching for the idea that would give you true freedom, entertain the idea that it's right under your very nose. Maybe it's a logistic problem you see it work, maybe it's in a product you use every day.

The point is, you don't necessarily need to be the next Elon Musk to make your mark as an entrepreneur. You don't have to design a ground-breaking electric car to change the world (although if that's your thing, more power to you!). All you really have to do is figure out a way to build a better mousetrap.

But how do you know your shiny new mouse-trap really is an improvement on the dull old original? Here's my litmus test for whether or not a business idea is viable: Can you say, with a fair amount of certainty, that the product or service you want to offer is inevitable? Is there such an obvious gap in this particular marketplace that someone is bound to fill it before long? If the answer to those questions is yes, then your idea is probably worth pursuing. You might have been the first person to think of it, or you might be the first person to be in a position to do something about it. Either way, it's inevitable that someone will develop this specific enterprise, so why shouldn't it be you? Remember what Walt Disney said: "If you can dream it, you can do it. Always remember that this whole thing was started with a dream, and a mouse."

You'd be surprised at how many of the random ideas you get on a daily basis have real business potential. That's why I advise keeping track of these passing notions in a notebook dedicated to your ideas. Much like the notebook where you jot down your goals, this journal will serve as a bank of inspiration whenever you're in need. The very first step in making something real is writing it down. Plus, recording these ideas, however briefly, guarantees that you'll remember them. Can you imagine what a different, better world we would live in if everybody acted upon their amazing, life-changing ideas the minute they had them? Too often we push these thoughts to the back of our heads, trying to make room for the more mundane issues that demand our attention (the mortgage, the laundry, the cat threw up again). The tragedy is that more often than not, we don't ever end up going back to those great ideas later. We simply forget about them. Write down your ideas before that can happen. What have you got to lose other than a little space in a notebook? Brian Tracy says the average person has four ideas in a year that could make them a millionaire. Fathom that for a moment. You had four plausible ideas last year that you could be enjoying and benefiting from this very moment. The only differences between the average person who becomes a millionaire and the average person who does not are bravery and the wherewithal to execute on their idea. That's literally it!

Here's a mental exercise I've shared with some of our colleagues and friends that always gets me going. I have brought you a genie lamp, and inside it is a business genie. He will grant you the one business wish that you have. He comes out of the lamp and you tell him the business idea you have and what success would look like for you. He says, "Your wish is granted. There is just one catch, however: You have to create a to-do list that will get the job done, and then you have to act on that list and execute the plan. If you complete each task on your list, your wish will be fulfilled." The idea here is that you can just about guarantee any accomplishment, if you're willing to do a bit of work. Pretend your success is absolutely going to happen, and work toward it. In a short period of time, you'll find a miracle has taken place. Others will call you lucky, and you can tell them all a genie did it. One thing's for certain: You miss 100 percent of the shots you don't take (and that includes Onyx shots).

Now, let's say for a moment that you know you'd like to begin the journey as an entrepreneur, but you're not sure what your idea or business would be. Maybe you haven't been paying attention to your million-dollar ideas or didn't write them down in a notebook. Let's imagine your goal is financial and personal freedom, and you'd like to leave your job. Your motivation might be to work from home and create your own schedule, or maybe you see the start of your business as a way to spend more time with family. If you don't have an idea just yet, don't worry. There's a new trend in entrepreneurship right now that revolves around the philosophy that you don't necessarily have to start a business with an idea. You can start a business with no ideas, with the answers lying all around you, especially in the right people. It's called "idea extraction." Everyone you work with, as well as your friends and your family, have complaints about the inefficiencies they deal with every day. Walk into any office and ask the person at the front desk what the most frustrating part of their day is. If one of your friends works at a law firm, doctor's office, or any other business that is located on every corner of every Main Street in America, ask them out for an Onyx Moonshine cocktail. Sit down with your notebook and interview them. After a short time, they'll tell you exactly what you might be able to create to make their life easier. Then, you can figure out how to systemize it and launch it as a business. Who knows, you might even be able to get the first customer to pay for it up-front, then sell the same product to additional businesses and grow. Sometimes, everyone is a potential customer. What do people want? When you see a pattern of need or want emerge, and filling that particular need is something you could be passionate about, then you may have just found your direction. So many successful companies have been launched as a result of the founder's frustration with something. Pete and I weren't able to buy a single spirit made in New England. It was frustrating to us that with such a rich heritage in distilling here, there wasn't a single product for sale. If you can find the frustration in any environment and fix it, you've just created your multimillion-dollar venture.

Considering that Pete and I had such a long-standing passion for spirits, it's funny that it took us as long as it did to figure out our destiny was in the drink. Looking back, I guess it's because we didn't really see an opportunity or place for us in the industry—until we noticed that the same four or five global, billion-dollar companies produced the vast majority of the spirits on the shelves.

The reason why these booze behemoths have such a monopoly over the American market dates all the way back to the end of prohibition. In 1933, when the ban against alcohol ended, the only distilleries and breweries that were capitalized well enough to get their factories up and running right away were owned by large, wealthy companies. The economic climate after prohibition essentially destroyed the American liquor industry by making it impossible for small, family-owned breweries and distilleries to get back in the game. It's interesting to note, by the way, that the income tax was established during prohibition to fill the revenue hole created by eliminating the tax associated with the sale of alcohol. Of course, after prohibition ended we were left with high alcohol tax *and* an income tax. Well played, government, well played.

Before prohibition, our country's spirits and beer market looked a lot like it does in Europe, South America, and other parts of the world, where different regions and communities each have their own family-owned distilleries and breweries that have been operating for generations. These homegrown businesses tend to have a commitment to quality that often gets lost when companies get too big, with families passing down and improving upon the necessary skills from generation to generation. Under these circumstances, spirits production is genuinely an art form—so it was nothing short of a tragedy that this creative, quality-centric approach was all but lost to Americans until the 1980s and 1990s when the craft movement began to grow.

By the time Pete and I were ready to launch Onyx in 2011, the market was already saturated with craft beers, and "handmade" tequilas and vodkas were getting more popular by the day. But there was still room for moonshine, and recognizing this Onyx-shaped gap in the market motivated us to get moving once and for all.

The other major motivating factor for us both was our family histories. Interestingly enough, neither Pete were fully aware of the fact that boot-legging was in our blood until we got the idea to make moonshine and started talking to family members. I knew about my family's speakeasy in the basement of Chaffee's Hotel in Middletown, but I didn't know that my ancestors were arrested in 1864 for shipping moonshine to Canada and not paying the tax, an unfortunate event that resulted in the collapse of Chafee & Company Distilling. We also didn't know that the farm owned by Pete's family in Wethersfield, Connecticut, had produced more than corn in its 100-year-plus history, if you catch my drift. Taking our personal histories into account, I find it kind of intriguing that Pete and I were compelled to make moonshine for a living before we even realized the depth of our connection to the stuff. Sure, we called ourselves the "moon-shiners" when we were sitting behind the board at Onyx Soundlab, but we were never even really sure why we chose the name. It's no surprise to me that scientists have discovered memories might be something that can be passed down from genera-tion to generation through our DNA.

So there we were, on the verge of stepping into an industry where small players had never really been active. Before 2000 there were exceptionally few people making whiskey or vodka or rum in a little distillery in a town somewhere; Diageo, Bacardi, Pernod Ricard, or Brown-Forman made virtually every spirit on the market. Pete and I recognized that the tide was shifting. We sensed and observed that there was a growing desire among consumers for things that were fresh, local, and tied to the history of their community. In these increasingly impersonal times, people want and need authenticity. But when we walked into liquor stores across New England and asked what local spirits they carried, we were told, "We don't carry any local booze."

Clearly, it was up to us to fill the void. But what would we make? As I said in Chapter 2, our investor wanted us to stick with tried and true options: vodka and limoncello. But he wasn't the only one who felt that way. Nearly every single liquor industry expert we asked for advice told us the same thing: "Vodka is the top-selling spirit" we heard over and over and over again. Top-selling spirit or not, Pete and I felt that the vodka market was very saturated. Every liquor store in every town is packed to the rafters with high-end vodka, low-end vodka, plain vodka, aggressively and ridiculously flavored vodka, organic vodka—you get the picture. Our market research also told us it looked as though vodka had peaked and was facing a potentially huge decrease in popularity based on its oversaturation for almost two decades. Many of these vodka brands are what we call vanity brands, owned by a celebrity who serves as a figurehead and subcontracts out to have the vodka made for them. As a result, all of these vodkas are really the same flavorless, odorless spirit from one bottle to the next to the next.

Deep down, Pete and I knew that moonshine was the spirit we wanted to make. But all those experts who told us to make vodka and/or limoncello convinced us they were right—for a period of time, at least. It wasn't necessarily that we agreed with their assessments (people think moonshine is poison; people think moonshine makes you go blind), but their concerns were enough to sufficiently freak us out. These people were supposed to be experts, right? What did we know, comparatively? We temporarily shelved the moonshine we'd been working on and set about designing a vodka of our very own. As for limoncello, we've always made an excellent version of the liqueur (if I do say so myself), sticking to an authentic Italian recipe we both researched the heck out of and enjoyed thoroughly in Italy. Even though we were reluctant to switch gears, we were also resolved to make the best of the situation, and of course, the best product we possibly could. So it definitely took the wind out of our sails when (as I mentioned in Chapter 2) another local limoncello company came from out of nowhere, beating us to the punch. There went our first-mover's advantage! And looking at the small area we'd marked for distribution, we knew there was no room for two local limoncellos. But as with so many "failures," the emergence of our competitor was a blessing in disguise because it prompted us to reevaluate—and by "re-evaluate," I mean "sit down with a bottle of moonshine and talk into the wee hours of the night." Over the course of that night, we realized we'd gotten completely sidetracked from our original mission, something that we allowed to happen when we stopped listening to our guts and started listening to other people. This other limoncello company was a warning sign from the universe, an omen that we were on the right track to begin with. So what if people think of moonshine as blindness-inducing back-woods swill? It was our job to redefine this truly

American spirit—the only truly American spirit besides bourbon. Within a week, we were refining our moonshine recipe, ordering glass bottles, and designing our now unmistakable label.

We wanted to do something authentically connected to our story, and to our area, and that was to make moonshine and, eventually, whiskey. Going further into that, we sensed at the time that we weren't the only ones out there looking to start down the moonshine trail. Talking to other people in our business, it became clear that there was about to be a great resurgence of moonshine. I think that kind of speaks to the power of zeitgeist. So we saw the moonshine movement coming, but through our binoculars at the time, it still seemed a safe distance away. We believed, when we started our venture, that we would be the very first legal moonshine to market. We were wrong.

Right before Onyx went to market, another moonshine company launched, one that was far more capitalized than we were, albeit located across the country. When I say capitalized, I mean capitalized enough to go national, right out of the gate. Bigger, however, is not always better. Personally, I think that the best model for a business is to do a year or two test run in a smaller market to prove that your product is viable; lucky for us, Connecticut is one of the best test markets in the country because we have so much socioeconomic diversity compacted into a relatively small geography (you can drive across Connecticut in an hour). From the shoreline and the cities to the boondocks to the Gold Coast, the range of interests, backgrounds, and means for such a small state is quite remarkable. I don't know why the other moonshine company chose a national launch, but I do know that ultimately it didn't matter because while they were technically selling "moonshine," their product was in fact nothing like ours. Packaged in a mason jar, this company went for kitschy. It hardly mattered that the liquor inside was nothing more than an inexpensive corn whiskey; the target market for their moonshine was novelty seekers, not connoisseurs, hipsters who wanted a trendy addition to their home bar or a funny gift to bring to a housewarming party in place of the usual bottle of Merlot. Right off the bat, Pete and I recognized that the majority of moonshine brands to come would be of this variety, so we decided to position Onyx as the only high-end moonshine on the market. From the luxury brand-inspired aesthetic of the label to the quality of the ingredients used in our recipe, everything about our product was meant to convey top-tier excellence: This is what great Gatsby drank. Would Gatsby drink anything out of a mason jar? Doubtful.

So while there wasn't enough room for two local limoncellos on the market, there was definitely enough room for more than one moonshine on the market—particularly because the market was brand new, and thus wide open. Because there weren't already multiple versions of moonshine on liquor store shelves, we had the freedom to carve out a space for ourselves right alongside the burgeoning novelty brands. And while our product was "new," in one sense, we weren't actually reinventing the wheel. In many ways, it falls into the category of being a small but significant tweak on an already-existing product. Moonshine is essentially just a clear, unaged whiskey. In fact, 150 years ago, moonshine was called whiskey—until people figured out that aging it in a barrel made a whole new product, what we call whiskey today. The invention of aged whiskey opened up the market for vodka, which didn't really exist in the United

States until after prohibition. It's worth noting that when Smirnoff was first introduced to this country in the 1950s, sales were very slow. Americans were accustomed to the taste of gin and brown spirits (whiskey and rum) and didn't know what to make of the clear, flavorless spirit. It wasn't until the company started using whiskey corks and began marketing vodka as a "white whiskey" with "no taste, no smell" that sales really took off. It was a home run for the liquor producers because vodka can be made quickly and inexpensively, with no aging needed. That meant lower production costs and higher profit margins.

The Smirnoff story is the perfect illustration of every entrepreneur's basic mission: Find a gap in the marketplace, fill it with something people didn't even know they wanted in the first place, and turn that product into a household staple.

The way we see it, at Onyx we're bringing back the real "white whiskey." Not only is Onyx a superior spirit to vodka, you're also supporting the American economy when you buy it. That's why, to me, Onyx really does represent the American dream: Anything they can make in any other country, we can make better—and we can make our world better in the process.

Not only is this piece of our business plan a critical part of our story, it also invades the minds and morale of our entire team. By innovating a new product in a new category, with a goal of reintroducing such a critical piece of American heritage, we're challenging the status quo while we go up against billion-dollar behemoths. The challenge is daunting, and a hell of a lot of fun. As we pick away at sales from the biggest spirits suppliers in the world, they're finding it very challenging to respond from a marketing and sales standpoint. Because no matter how hard they try, consumers want authentic, craft, and handmade, and you just fake that when you're a billion-dollar business. They will, however, continue trying, and they have the resources to back it up. I saw what I thought was an equally brilliant and mortifying commercial by Budweiser at the 2015 Super Bowl. We're all aware of the rapidly growing popularity of craft breweries and beers in the United States. There's likely one open within 10 miles of you as you read this. As a result, Budweiser has had a dip in sales and market share, and the new young customers that are reaching drinking age are gravitating away from this tried-and-true American brand. However, they also have a substantial brand loyalty, especially from the older consumers that have been drinking it their entire lives and find new craft brands inaccessible. So Bud released a high-energy commercial called "Brewed the Hard Way." You can watch it on YouTube. They created the term "macro beer" in opposition to the popularity of *micro beers*. They actually say, "Let them drink their pumpkin peach ale." It's hilarious and most certainly created an even bigger hatred for the brand from the hipsters and micro-beer connoisseurs that only drink craft beers. The interesting thing in this study is that those drinkers are not going to be converted over to Budweiser anyway. So was this a brilliant marketing coup that inspires their loyal base to keep buying, or the most effective way to piss off a group of new customers that the corporate world has ever seen? I don't know the answer, although the commercial has 10–1 thumbs down to thumbs up on YouTube. I know the craft beer industry scoffed at it as incredibly insulting.

What I think we can take from this is that as you develop you business venture, you will invariably face fierce competition in your market from those market leaders you'll be taking sales from. But no matter how much capital you have, you still can't buy authenticity, and you can't buy a true emotional following from your customers. You have to earn it. And once you do, it should be the one asset you protect more than any other thing you've got.

Sangaree

1 oz. Onyx Moonshine
4 oz. ruby port
1 tsp. sugar or simple syrup
2 thin lemon wheels

Add ingredients to a shaker with ice and shake vigorously. Strain into a glass and top with freshly grated nutmeg.

Before sangria there was sangaree, a colonial concoction made with port and fresh fruit. The addition of Onyx Moonshine rounds out the flavors and brings this cocktail into the 21st century.

◈ CHAPTER 8 ◈

SNOOZE YOU LOSE, BOOZE YOU WIN

Seizing Opportunity Before It's Too Late

If losing our chance at being the first legal moonshine on the market taught us anything, it was that he who hesitates is truly lost when it comes to starting a business. That's why once you zero in on exactly what gap in the marketplace your venture is destined to fill, you've got to strike while the iron is hot—particularly if, like us, you have the sense that your product or service is inevitable. It's all about tuning into the zeitgeist, then finding a way to differentiate your offering from the rest.

Distinguishing ourselves from the other, more novelty-oriented moonshines on the market was easy. Well, not easy—it was, and continues to be, a tremendous effort. But our path was clear, thanks to our moonshine's remarkably unique characteristics: Most important, it's smoother than any other moonshine on the market; it's also from New England, a region people associate with America's founding and heritage; and the marketing and branding around our moonshine are ultra-premium, something else nobody associates with moonshine. But best of all is the unique story we have to tell, one that gives those unique characteristics context and helps us establish an authentically personal relationship with our customers. To further entrench ourselves and the brand, we will be substantially growing the production of our Secret Stash whiskey, recognizing there is massive demand surging for American whiskey in foreign markets.

It doesn't matter if you're opening up a cupcake shop, or starting a software company, or making the next craft beer or organic wine—you've got to have an intriguing story. Even more important, you've got to understand how to effectively tell that story. I've talked a little bit about the fact that Onyx does almost no traditional advertising whatsoever. That's because we've found that developing a good relationship with the media results in better, more effective publicity, at virtually no cost. Part of the reason why this is true is that the return of investment on traditional advertising is getting smaller and smaller. This is no surprise when you consider the fact that people are bombarded with advertisements nearly every minute of every day. Spend a half hour in any major city and look around; ads literally cover every surface, never mind spending a couple minutes on whatever social media you're into. Advertising has become so pervasive in our society that it's practically meaningless. Robert Stephens, the founder of Geek Squad, said it best: "Advertising is the tax you pay for being unremarkable." So how does an entrepreneur with limited funds combat this and create an effective marketing plan that has a quick ROI (return on investment)? The answer lies in authenticity and in being remarkable for reasons that will resonate with consumers. Contemporary customers crave authenticity because it's becoming so rare! Think about it: In the United States, the greedy drive to maximize profits has had a devastating effect on pretty much everything that's available for us to easily purchase. Clothes are ruined after being worn for just a few months. Furniture breaks after a few years, whereas back in the day it was passed on for generations. We pay hundreds of dollars for bottle service in a nightclub, drinking some mass-produced swill that was made by a machine—and the glass bottle actually costs more than the contents. Even our food is so unauthentic it's actually harming us with creepy preservatives, unnatural additives, and coloring. Why is all this happening? Because many companies that provide us with these luxury goodies we should be so fortunate to have are led by extremely efficient, profit-oriented MBAs beholden to their shareholders and forced to deliver profits quarterly or risk losing their jobs. It's profit over people, pure and simple—and it's affecting our health and our wallets. But the trends are showing that consumers are demanding authenticity more than ever, and the corporations will have to respond appropriately if they're to stay viable. And while they spend years trying to move their massive bureaucracies into a new strategic direction, guess what you can be doing? Giving the customers exactly what they want, like, tomorrow. And the fun part is, those customers will happily give you money for it.

Before consumers spend their hard-earned dollars on whatever it is you're selling, they want some kind of tangible proof that it's going to be worth it. As a new venture, it's likely that you're often going to have to make them switch from whatever you were buying before, and that can be a challenge. People don't like change. You're really ahead of the game if you can also cause those consumers to feel an *emotional* connection to what you're offering them. The grocery chain Whole Foods is a great example of that. By creating a more holistic environment for shopping, customers happily pay more for products. They're growing like mad and I recently heard they're going to be launching a less-expensive line of grocery stores (my first thought was *That's every other grocery store, but okay*). I'll share another example of an interesting startup company I discovered. For Christmas this past year, I asked for a watch. I needed a nice watch that would pair well with my suits but also shines in a pair of overalls and a some work boots (just kidding). I found a brand called Brathwait whose slogan, "Return of the Gentleman," emotionally connected with me. I discovered them through my social media feed. I was initially attracted by the actual design of the watch. It had a large white face with simple numbering and a stunning Italian calf leather band. It was minimalistic, was elegant, and featured some spectacular photos that really helped it sparkle. It led me to their social media page, where I learned a little more about them and discovered that the company was inspired by historical poet Richard Brathwait. Thought to be London's first gentleman, he published *The Complete Guide to the English Gentleman* in 1631. I was fascinated by the story. As I dug further still, I found their pricing was extremely affordable for what I thought was reasonable to spend. Finally, I discovered they employ "transparent marketing," whereby they share their full cost to purchase the raw materials and assemble the watch, then their markup. By removing the middleman (retailers) and selling direct to the public, they avoid distribution and retailer markups and can maintain a fair price that they're willing to share with the customers. I loved the transparency and felt they weren't marking up exorbitantly based just on marketing and pictures. A few days later, I received my watch in the mail for $150, and have shared the story with quite a few people who have asked about it. So let's think about this for a moment:

1. They engaged me through great product design and social media marketing.
2. They had a fascinating story with true history.
3. They helped me to understand their business model, demonstrated their pricing, and proudly showed me how their passing savings directly to me— that otherwise I would have had to pay.

Ultimately, they gained a customer who was willing to part with my pennies, who was emotionally engaged with the brand, and who's gone on to be a brand advocate. Textbook!

You can have all of the above around your plan, but you'll remember the first thing I said as part of the last anecdote: I saw the watch on my social media feed. Had they not been able to reach me and tell me about the product, I would have gone somewhere else. You could have the cure to stupid, but if no one knows, it doesn't matter because they won't buy it from you. That's where the media comes in. An unbiased article in a newspaper or magazine lends far more credibility to the value of your product or service than a full-page advertisement in the same publication; a mention on the local news about your exciting new business is a million times more engaging than a spot during the commercial break (which is also expensive). That's why I always say if there's one skill every entrepreneur should master, it's the art of writing a press release—or paying someone else to! Every journalist, every reporter—whether in print, online, or TV—has a quota of stories each and every day that need to be filled. If you can engage them with a well-written press release, not only are you making their job easier, you've just gotten yourself a bunch of free publicity for being remarkable. Be newsworthy, and no advertising tax for you!

Once we were up and running, it didn't take long for us to dominate the local media scene in terms of them wanting interviews; soon after that, national outlets came calling. To date, Onyx has been featured on NBC News, CBS News, National Public Radio (which reaches more than 20 million listeners), Bloomberg, even the front page of *Time Magazine*'s Website. A variety of high-profile newspapers, magazines, and Websites have also run articles about Onyx, including the *New York Times*. And of course, we always love brainstorming new ways to get the word out there while having a lot of fun. Pete and I hosted our own radio show on The Rock 106.9 WCCC (the radio station famous for giving Howard Stern his start) called *The Moonshine Report* that reached between 100,000 and 125,000 listeners all over the world. It was fun; it was authentic; it was real. We'd go on the air with a station DJ, mix up a bunch of cocktails live, get silly, and chat about making Onyx and fun events or parties coming up. Customers loved it, and they listened because it wasn't an ad; it was just Adam and Pete from Onyx Moonshine being silly. Once you get that free publicity ball rolling, it's nearly impossible to stop it! Buzz leads to more buzz, and that buzz leads to opportunities for your business to grow, sometimes in ways you never even expected. Like the time we were in the radio station and had the opportunity to meet the band Pop Evil, whose single "Deal with the Devil" hit number one on the Billboard charts in 2014. The band's latest album just happened to be called "Onyx," which gave us the perfect excuse to introduce them to our moonshine. That day, we went to the gun range all day and shot thousands of rounds with them. Then they hosted us at their concert at the Mohegan Sun Casino, where we wrapped up the night drinking Onyx Moonshine. We loved their music and what they'd created, and they loved Onyx—so much, in fact, that they decided to feature bottles of Onyx in their music video for the song "Torn to Pieces," which as of this writing has a total of almost 5 million views on YouTube, and also went to the top of the Billboard charts. A small business here in Connecticut, Hardcore Sweet Cupcakes, used Onyx in their Cherry Moonshine Pie Cupcake, and that cupcake went on to win an episode of Food Network's *Cupcake Wars* hosted by rock star Rob Zombie. That's amazingly powerful advertising that was essentially completely free. All we had to do was harness the energy behind our brand and keep telling the story; the law of momentum allows everything else to just keep happening. It also does help that we're in the liquor business, and sending some bottles of free product is always a great introduction.

One of the most amazing examples of this sort of snowball effect was the inclusion of Onyx in the official gift bags for the 54th annual Grammy Awards—a tremendous coup for a startup from Connecticut. We were fortunate to have a contact at the company that selects the products to go in the gift bags every year who was really engaged by the story of Onyx and thought we'd make a unique addition to the top-dollar swag. Actually, we were more than fortunate. Most brands pay top dollar for the privilege of being included in the gift bags presented to celebrities at award shows like the Oscars, Grammys, and Emmys; we only had to pay a very nominal fee (so small I don't even remember what it was) and ship a bunch of product. It was actually more expensive for us to ship the bottles to California for the red carpet event! Still, knowing that 160 of the music industry's biggest stars went home that night with a bottle of Onyx was worth every penny.

One of those celebrities, Seth MacFarlane (actor, voice actor, animator, screenwriter, producer, film director, singer, and creator of the TV show *Family Guy*), became an Onyx fan and we ended up shipping a supply to him for a party in Beverly Hills. As a thank-you, he sent back a Ted doll (the talking teddy bear from the movie *Ted* that MacFarlane wrote, directed, and starred in alongside Mark Wahlberg), which we then photographed on our bottling line. The photo blew up on social media (the Ted bear working a moon-shine bottling line? How could it not?), resulting in still more publicity.

Speaking of social media, platforms like Facebook, Twitter, Pinterest, and Instagram are invaluable tools when it comes to generating free press for your brand. There are new plat-forms about to launch any time, all of which you should be sure to stay on top of. It goes back to the point of the growing consumer desire for hand-made quality and organic stories. Word of mouth is better than anything, and social media is how word of mouth spreads in our world today. I'd rather people hear about Onyx moonshine from a buddy than anything else in the world. Think about it: Are you more likely to buy a bottle of booze because you saw an ad for it in a magazine or because your best friend posts a picture of him enjoying a glass on Facebook, or better yet, has it on his bar at home? Word of mouth is the most hon-est and most valuable way to grow—and it's free! As soon as we recognized the vast brand-building potential of social media, we set to work grow-ing our presence. Feeding the social media beast is such an important, daily effort that we quickly realized we needed to hire somebody full time to manage social media, so we merged our events department with social media and hired one talented individual to handle it all. If whatever business venture you're planning doesn't have social media as a critical component of your marketing plan, you're entirely missing the boat. The thing I like most about social media is that advertisement-style posts don't even perform that well. People like authentic content. They like to learn, hear from you, and engage. I think this force of authenticity and true human engagement is the best part about it. We get to actually hear from our customers, and they from us. It's like having access to a constant focus group, in addition to all the other promotional benefits. Combining our social media and promotional events efforts into one role made a lot of sense for us as we really needed someone to handle both on a full-time basis. The combination makes perfect sense: Both promotional events and social media are forms of grassroots, guerilla-style marketing. And believe me, we put just as much effort into our promotional events as we do our social media presence. We've held hundreds of tastings at farmers markets, liquor stores, restaurants, and bars, introducing Onyx to thousands of potential customers and sellers. Because it's not just the people buying your product that you want on your side. You also want to actively court the people who'll be bringing your brand to the masses. Get to know the cashiers, the bartenders, the mixologists. Talk to them one-on-one and find out what's going to really motivate them to push your product over one of the many, many others they could sell instead.

Think of these individuals as brand ambassadors. Make sure they're well informed about your product and impressed with its quality. Of course, our events aren't limited to farmers market tastings; in fact, Onyx has become known for throwing uniquely over-the-top promotional affairs like "The Great Gatsby Onyx Moonshine Ball & Onyx 111 Infusion Challenge," a "cocktail showdown" pitting 15 city restaurants against each other in a 1920s-themed gala at the historic Wadsworth Mansion in Middletown, Connecticut. The gala was a sold-out event with more than 300 guests in attendance, not to mention a total blast! Thanks to our early promotional efforts, by the day we were legal to sell and deliver Onyx moonshine, we had a huge preorder list through social media. To be sure, when that day came, after a year and a half of planning, the consumer demand was greater than we could have imagined. In the first 48 hours we were "open" for business, we sold more than 50 cases of Onyx—and it was all due to the immediate demand created through social media and a well-written press release. We were able to spin our unique story into 3 straight weeks of media coverage, which drove up our social media numbers, which attracted still more press—you get the picture. It's a never-ending cycle, unlike an ad that runs and is immediately forgotten. The connections you make on social media have the potential to last forever.

The result of all this work was that we created real and genuine pull for our product, and nothing in the world is more valuable than pull. It almost makes you invincible; at the very least, it greases the wheels of the machine. Allow me to explain how. Every industry is slightly different, of course, but the high-level principles are the same. In the liquor industry model we, as the producer, are the supplier. We sell to the distributor (trucks, warehouses, and salespeople), who sells to the retailer (liquor stores and restaurants/bars), who then sells to the final customer, the consumer. The typical, unremarkable model is that the supplier does everything they can to *push* the product through to the final consumer. This means convincing and incentivizing the distributors to place your product into stores and restaurants—which can be a challenge because they are selling a lot of products from many, many producers. Of course, the big producers have the big brands, and by the very nature of the model, the distributors are beholden to the suppliers that move the most product because that's tied directly to their revenue. Then, you have the distributors selling the product into the retailers. Convincing the liquor stores to create shelf real estate for the product comes next, as does convincing bartenders and restaurateurs to put it on the highly coveted back bar and crossing their fingers for a cocktail menu placement. Last, assuming the proper education went down the chain correctly, the product is in the right place, and the retailers are willing to help actually sell it, you hope to get a sale from a consumer. The whole thing can be quite tedious and involves everyone cooperating—think herding cats. I don't want to lose you, so stay with me! Now, here's where the magic happens: a complete reversal of the model, where we as the supplier focused entirely on the end consumer. Remember when I touched on the Grammy Awards, press releases, and getting lots of free media to leverage that against social media when we were just launching? The result from that campaign was all the consumers were going to their liquor stores and asking for the product on their own initiative. We created demand from the product on the consumer end having never spoken with a distributor or more than one single retailer. The pull created by our creative marketing initiatives grabbed the attention of the retailers, who only really ever ordered from distributors. And so, the store owners and bartenders were all asking their distributors how they can order this Onyx Moonshine all the customers were calling about. The distributors had no idea! Over some months, the distributors started courting us, when usually it's the other way around. We had our pick of distributors because they saw they didn't have to do as much work to build our brand from scratch. The pull was already there! The result was a better negotiation and a better partner from the get-go.

Think about some companies you know that have such strong natural pull, they almost never advertise. Apple is a great one that comes to mind, as is Facebook. When was the last time you saw a Facebook ad? In the liquor business, one really renowned whiskey brand is Pappy van Winkle. They have been around a very long time and produce limited amounts of their whiskey. Because their pull is far greater than their production, they very, very rarely advertise. When devising the plan for your company, I think I've proven the point that the obsession with the final customer (as well as finding uniquely innovative ways to reach them) should be the cornerstone of your marketing plan. Forget the advertising plan. Create a pull plan!

Last, your goal should be to make a long-term customer, not a sale. It's easy to get a sale, and it's not that hard to get a customer. It's much harder to keep one. By finding creative ways to continue engaging with your customers, to help them "discover" you and spread the word, you'll create a market of brand champions that will keep the cash flow rolling *and* grow your business.

Sidecar

1 1/2 oz. Onyx Moonshine
1/4 oz. cognac
1/2 oz. Cointreau or orange liqueur
3/4 oz. fresh lemon juice

Shake all ingredients over ice. Strain and garnish with an orange twist.

Want to impress the bartender? Order a Sidecar with Onyx Moonshine.

CHAPTER 9

THE ENTREPRENEUR'S DILEMMA

Weighing the Pros and Cons of Micromanaging a "Small Business" Versus Big-Picture Thinking

As entrepreneurs, it's our job to think big. Ideas are the currency we deal in, the lifeblood of our hopes and dreams. Part of the process of becoming a successful entrepreneur is figuring out how to tune into your ideas and instincts and, as we talked about, trusting your gut over the (sometimes-misplaced) guidance of others. All of this is crucial when it comes to launching your unique, authentic enterprise. That said, even the most skilled innovators don't necessarily have what it takes when it comes to the nuts and bolts of taking an already lucrative business to the next level. So it's just as crucial to know when it's time to step back and hire expert managers who can help to propel your company's profitability rate through the stratosphere.

I'll share a short story with you that really brings home the point about how detrimental you can be to your own business, after you've worked so hard to set it up and let it flourish. As I mentioned previously, one of the businesses I set up was with my Uncle Brian. He was a fantastically gifted, hardworking entrepreneur with a passion for building and restoring really fast muscle cars. The business I helped him set up started shipping rare muscle car parts via eBay and morphed over a year or so into an full-on classic and muscle car restoration company. My job was primarily marketing and helping to set up the businesses processes so it could function. The challenge was, my uncle was as OCD as it gets. Anal doesn't begin to describe it. As such, there was very little he would delegate to others because he didn't believe they could do the job, or at least, do the job to his standards. As a result, he worked the equivalent of two men, staying until the wee hours to paint a car just right, or coming in early Sunday morning to sweep correctly. The result was a business that was prosperous, as clients saw a passion in him that was rare in the business. His pride in the work the shop did gave customers a true sense of authenticity and raw, exceptional quality. So they came from all over the country. However, the inability to "let go" of the business caused riffs, not only in our family, but also among the staff. Employee turnover was high, revenue was unstable, and his health deteriorated from the intensity of it all. Then, he was told he had a bad form of cancer with potentially only months to live. After discussions with my aunt and cousin, and many late-night phone conversations with me, he walked away from the business entirely and moved for a period of time down to Florida. Unfortunately, it was too late, and he passed away soon after. What's interesting is that as soon as he moved to Florida, the business began to prosper in a new kind of way. Without his daily micromanaging, the systems that were put in place took over, and the business as its own entity was able to truly grow. Of course, my aunt was there to guide and manage it, but she was much less emotionally involved in it than he was, and as a result, it was better run. Sales actually doubled from 2012 to 2014, literally from less oversight.

This eventuality is something to keep in mind right from the very beginning, something Pete and I did not do. When an entrepreneur launches any business, no matter how small, one of the best assets they can think about gaining is the formation of an advisory board. You need to hear a voice that's not inside your head and not your business partner. They will tell you the hard truths and help you think about the things that most certainly will happen. Your advisors can add perspective to opportunities or even help you see how a challenge is not a challenge. The advisory board can be informal to start. Essentially, what you're looking for are successful people, preferably in your industry of choice. You want to have a team of people standing by who've already done what you're trying to do, who've made the mistakes you're bound to make. Ideally, the people on this board should be diverse in terms of their expertise, with proven track records in a range of areas (finances, manufacturing, marketing, and so on). Don't be shy about approaching entrepreneurs you admire, even if you don't necessarily know them personally. The worst somebody can say is *no*! I'm fortunate to serve as chair on the board of the Viscogliosi Entrepreneurship Center, which supports entrepreneurs in the Greater Hartford area. My experiences have taught me that one of the great things about so many entrepreneurs is that they understand the struggle of startups and tend to be really passionate about helping entrepreneurs succeed. Hell, that's why I wrote this book. It's the cycle of mentorship: Have mentors, become a mentor. The fact is, most novice business types simply don't have the experience and knowledge necessary to reach their goals and milestones, and that's okay. In fact, this naïveté might even end up helping to boost your business in more ways than one. Once again, it all goes back to that all-important adage: *Ask for advice, you'll get money; ask for money, you'll get advice.* The successful advisors you seek out will probably be the first in line to either help fund you or connect you to people who can help you to raise capital. Naturally, you don't want to go into the relationship with the sole purpose of looking for money. But I've found that if you approach potential sources of help with a genuine interest in listening to what they have to say and getting to know them as people, chances are they'll offer both guidance and resources. Every single person on the Onyx board of advisors has, at some point or another, either loaned us money, invested in our company, or helped us to find other investors. Even some of our customers, from restaurant owners to bartenders, have introduced us to other investors. That's the power of building a solid network of friends, advisors, and customers.

I'll admit that I'm not a huge fan of structured networking events. More often than not, these formal events end up being a complete waste of time, not to mention money. I have quite literally never found one of these tedious occasions to be productive. While everyone in attendance is preoccupied by the singular (and singularly unappealing) motive of self-promotion, it's challenging to make any real progress. When everybody's talking and pitching, nobody's listening. So instead of squandering precious hours and funds on networking events where the only thing you'll get is pocket full of business cards, just get out there and have fun! Seek out non-profits and other foundations that mean something to you, and support their cause by donating your product or service to their events. Go volunteer to help the community somehow; volunteer for some boards on organizations that intrigue you. This more organic form of networking is both a way to give back and a way to spread the word about your business, while showing people that you're about more than just making money for yourself. In the process, the contacts will come, and the relationships you establish will be genuine. You'll get real results because you've put yourself in the right position to do so.

Organic networking is also an ideal way to find potential members of your team. As an entrepreneur, you're most likely a skilled creator with a gift for big ideas, but you might not be the right person to oversee the real nuts and bolts, day-to-day production of your project long term—and that's okay. Play to your strengths. Figure out which area of your business is the best suited to your particular talents, and invest your time and energy there. The most important piece of your business after you've prototyped your idea and service is, without a doubt, the quality of your team. You're only as good as the quality of those around you. Renowned businessman Jim Rohn said it best: "You are the average of the five people you spend the most time with." Because you'll be working—a lot—make that average the best you can! Much as you might want to oversee every last detail of your project, you simply cannot do it all effectively. As Teddy Roosevelt put it, "The best executive is the one who has sense enough to pick good men to do what he wants done, and self-restraint enough to keep from meddling with them while they do it."

It's your team that's going to make up for all the weaknesses you have as an entrepreneur, and believe me, you have plenty. We all do. The ability to seek out the right people to propel your business is a skill unto itself, and one that can take years to hone. Recognize who it is you would ideally have advising you, and do everything within your power to connect with those people. Recognizing this is incredibly freeing to the mind and takes a load of stress off your shoulders. Once you realize that all the people who can help you create exactly the reality you want already exist in the world, you can then spend your time building a team that will be more effective instead of trying to teach yourself skills that could take years to develop. If you're an entrepreneur, focus on being an entrepreneur, damn it! We applied this principle directly to our space launch project. Our vision was to launch a bottle of Onyx Moonshine into space, on a silver platter, with a rocks glass. We knew a custom platform would have to be built, and that there was a whole bunch of science to get done. Did we sit down and try to understand the scientific principles behind building a platform to be fastened to a 30-foot aeronautical weather balloon, then lifted 22 miles up into space, all while being filmed with a bunch of GoPro cameras? Hell no. So we jumped on the Google and spent some time looking for help. We located a Connecticut physics guru named Ray Cirno who had been featured in the news for his successful balloon launches. He already did the work, knew the process, and volunteered to help us complete our crazy project. Find the team, excite them with a challenge, and get to work! We've already set a new horizon and are crafting plans to send a bottle of Onyx, shall we say, even further away—I'll keep you in suspense for now on that one. This project has even spawned talk of our starting a new, unique venture that involves space exploration. Great teams build great futures. After you have your product or idea, focus your energy on building a team around you that can successfully bring the idea to fruition. This is literally why God made scientists.

One thing Pete and I learned the hard way is that it's never too early to put together that informal board of advisors, a precursor to the more formal board of directors you'll likely convene once you're really growing and ready to bring in some big-time investors. The difference between the two can basically be summed up as follows: A board of advisors is a somewhat-casual assembly of mentors, generally with industry-specific knowledge, who are willing to offer their guidance, usually for nothing in return. The advisory board is more informal, with the members typically not having any actual voting power. The group can be as informal as a few friends you call occasionally, or organized to meet on occasion to conduct a more structured conversation. A board of directors is a more formal collection of people who have the power to approve or disapprove the decisions you make as the head of your company. Generally, it's the duty of the board of directors to protect the interests of the shareholders. When you're creating a more formal board of advisors and/or directors, bear in mind that the members will likely expect either shares in your company or some type of stipend. That's okay, because one thing's for sure: Once you start demanding more of people, you really want to make sure they're both adequately incentivized and compensated. (Just remember to be both careful and generous with equity.) If you've assembled a rock-star group of advisors, they will bring an incredible value to your company through their advice, experience, and network. Here's when you ask yourself. Do you want 100 percent of something that will be very small, or a much smaller percentage of something that will be extremely big? It's very hard to do big on your own, and I love big—so I vote the latter.

In my opinion, everyone should have an advisory board. If the task of assembling one sounds overwhelming, consider this: You may already have an advisory board and not even know it! If you're a startup and you have a few people you go to often with questions, well, guess what? They're your advisory board. If you're at the point where you're growing your business and want to get more formal with your advisory board, that's just as beneficial.

On our advisory board, we have quite an eclectic group of people, including successful professionals from the software, finance, and beverage industries; one member is even an Onyx distributor. We like the idea of having a diverse group of minds with different specialties to help guide us along the way. Not only do our advisory members help offer advice on strategy when we need it, but because many of them have brokered business deals ranging from small to enormous, they're also able to advise us on growth, capital raising, and terms. In all honesty, considering advisory board members are free for the most part, it would be stupid not to get one going right away.

When your advisory board becomes more formal, you also want to make sure to set clear expectations for the amount of time and effort you'll need from them. Consider creating a schedule for board meetings, anywhere from once a month (for startups) to quarterly for more established businesses. When it comes to the meetings themselves, have a very well-thought-out agenda and make sure all the members have it ahead of time. There are a wealth of books and other resources available with tips for how to get the most out of your business meetings. I encourage you to seek them out!

Other very important points to consider when putting your board together: If you can get access to well-known names in your industry (for us, this would be someone like the CEO of a major global spirits company), this will carry a lot of weight with future investors, especially venture capital people or banks. Plus, this alliance will open up access to potential funding from that executive's company and potential partnership opportunities, and could even lead to an eventual exit conversation (if that's a direction you want to take your company). By the way, when I refer to an "exit," I'm talking about selling your company and removing yourself from the picture.

This process of seeking out like-minded expert managers and colleagues is never-ending. Even now, Pete and I are in a position where we're going to have to locate some very skilled talent in the spirit industry, particularly in production and sales, in order to expand. Three years into our venture, we need to focus on three things: vision, control, and management. To do that, we need to hire exceptionally skillful individuals capable of building a solid upper-level management team. But even in terms of day-to-day operations at the startup level, you truly can't afford to hire talent that's not up to the job. It will cost you time and money. I've hired people who ended up not being the right fit because I hadn't quite nailed down the specific requirements of their positions, and these mistakes cost us both time and money. I'm also not a micromanager at all. We work very hard to train new members of our team, set expectations that are lofty but reasonable, and then give them the space to succeed.

The part of my job that I loathe the most is anytime I have to let somebody go. Sometimes it's unavoidable, particularly because in the context of a start-up, you might not have the time (and you certainly don't have the experience) to fully articulate the responsibilities and long-term goals of each particular role within the company—especially if they're evolving and employees need to wear many different hats. The problem is, when you don't fully articulate those responsibilities and goals, it might be your fault that your employees are not succeeding—not theirs. So you really want to create a situation where everyone you hire has the potential to find great success. Your hiring philosophy should start there. Always remember: If your employees are successful, you're successful. As their leader, it's your job to give them access to the resources they need to thrive on their own terms, without you having to micromanage them. Help people understand your vision, and what success would look like for them within the role you hired them to perform—but for the most part, leave the rest up to them. We're always there to guide our employees on that journey to professional fulfillment, but we make sure they're the ones behind the wheel. I want them to own their work, and I want to celebrate with them when they've won. Whether you plan on staying at the helm of your business for the rest of your life or envision yourself handing over the reins at some point in the future, your goal should be to set your company up to run and be successful without you. You need freedom to truly thrive and operate as a successful entrepreneur. In order to do that you need to have a team of people who are as enthusiastic about your mission as you are. Your employees need to feel independent in order to own their success. Think about it: Have you ever been able to do a job well when your boss was hovering over your shoulder, expecting you to screw up at every turn? It's like Horace Mann said: "You may be liberal in your praise where praise is due: It costs nothing; it encourages much." Positive reinforcement is an incredibly important part of empowering your team. So many people don't feel appreciated at work.

Just this morning, we had a huge mess at the factory. The ceiling leaked water, and there was an enormous puddle on the floor when everybody showed up to work. Except by the time I got there, it was gone. Our distiller, Kent, cleaned it up all on his own, without having to be asked. I always say that the mark of a good team member is if they stop and pick up a piece of garbage on the floor at work without having to be asked. Of course, even good employees aren't necessarily the right employees. That turned out to be the case with one person we hired. This particular individual was a very hard worker and, to an extent, very good at what he did. But he was someone who needed a fairly significant amount of direction and structure to really flourish. Now, as I said, I'm not a micromanager, and because the company was still new and small, there weren't a lot of systems or a particularly solid infrastructure at that time. Without those guideposts in place, this worker wasn't as able to be as successful as his abilities would have allowed him. It became increasingly clear to us mutually that he would do better in a company with more structure, and that his job with Onyx was holding him and us back. So as difficult as it was to sit this person down and tell him how we felt, it had to be done. Serendipitously, we were able to find our employee a job in sales with our distributor, so he continues to sell our product in a situation where his employers and their systems are very formalized and he has all the administrative support he needs. We all ended up getting the best of both worlds, and I learned that I needed to refine my requirements for that particular position.

Basically, it boils down to this: If you're approaching your position as an employer from a standpoint of genuinely caring for others and wanting everybody around you to be successful, not make you successful, then success will come to you organically. If you have an employee who's not performing well for you, they're probably not performing well for themselves. You need to sit down with that employee and say, "I care for you. I care for your success. Let's figure out the best way to get you there." Remember: The best military leaders are the ones who would truly die for their troops and lead from the front. I can't emphasize enough the importance of hiring and planning your team very carefully. They are the pieces that make your machine run, and they are also family. Every time I read a news article about some company that risked their employees' lives in a potentially avoidable mining accident or some other terrible disaster, I can't help but think about the sense of responsibility that any entrepreneur or CEO has when leading an organization. If you're not doing this for your customers and your team, who are you doing it for? Yourself? How shortsighted and boring. If you can get to a place where your top priorities are your customers and your team, everything else should unfold perfectly for you. That's another way to make the world a better place!

Cinna-Moon

2 oz. Onyx Moonshine Cape Cod Cranberry
2 oz. Fireball Cinnamon Whiskey

Add ingredients to a shaker over ice. Strain on to fresh ice, and top with a splash of club soda.

Cranberry and cinnamon aren't just autumn flavors. Whip up this cocktail anytime you feel nostalgic for falling leaves and toasty fires!

CHAPTER 10

SOCIALLY CONSCIOUS COMMERCE

*How Your Business Can Make the World
a Better Place*

When we think of the stereotypical entrepreneur throughout history, we don't always imagine the most benevolent of figures. The first thing many of us picture is a wealthy old man with a monocle and top hat, chomping on a cigar as he ruthlessly enslaves workers in his factory; picture a more nefarious version of the Monopoly man. Historically, that image of the cartoonishly immoral industrialist gives way to the greed-crazed, cold-blooded banker of the 1980s typified by Patrick Bateman in

American Psycho (which is not to say that all bankers are serial killers—I guess). But although times haven't changed entirely—the wealthiest people in our state, for example, are hedge-fund managers, who basically make money when other people lose money—I've observed a highly encouraging trend in start-up companies over the past few years: a reflection, in mission and practice, of the relatively recent recognition that the world is a very small place, and as human beings, it's our responsibility to make it better. More and more entrepreneurs are finding ways to be inspired by this responsibility, looking at areas of our civilization that are in need of repair and innovation, and responding with smart, impactful business. Whether it's a "cleantech" company focused on finding renewable resources to power our lives, or a clothing label that uses only recycled materials, or even a manufacturer that donates a portion of its proceeds to charities like Feed the Children, entrepreneurs are finally accepting their place in the universe as change-makers. What's miraculous is that for the first time in human history, the dollars and prosperity are really beginning to follow the positive businesses. And regardless of their particular industry, every single businessperson can take part in helping to drive this initiative forward.

At Onyx, one thing we feel really strongly about is helping our employees to work healthier. Healthy employees are happy employees, and happy employees are productive employees. To that end, we allow all of our employees as much vacation time as they want. (What's that? You want to fill out an application?) This might sound like a risky offering for us to make, and we do impose very slight limitations this policy—there are a couple of incredibly busy times during the year when we need to have the entire team on board, for example—but in general, we find that our employees don't abuse this privilege. Sometimes, I have to encourage them to leave. I believe this is because when you treat people with the respect they deserve, they show you the same. Because they're in control of their success and the success of the business, they own it like we do.

Another somewhat-nontraditional policy at Onyx is our flexibility regarding working from home. Some employers seem to be afraid that letting their employees work from home will lead to lots of loafing on the company dime, but we find that when it comes to our staff that's not involved in production, allowing them to work remotely when they want to results in a higher, not lower, rate of productivity. Members of our team are required to be on-site for scheduled meetings or other special events, but otherwise, if somebody wants to work from their sun porch wearing a pair of old pajamas, that's perfectly fine with me. As long as employees are ethical, stay on brand, and stick to the values of the company, I don't care how the job gets done—just that it gets done!

It comes down to this: If you've chosen your employees well and you believe that you can trust them, show that you care about their well-being. Model a relaxed mindset. Operate from a place of calm, knowing that your team can and will perform at the top of their game. For me, genuinely caring about your team is part of sustainable entrepreneurship. Without your team, you have nothing as an entrepreneur. The next part of sustainable entrepreneurship involves giving back on a larger scale, even if you're just showing support for your local community. At Onyx, we donated either products, funds, or both to more than 200 nonprofits last year. We're able to justify these expenditures financially because it's good for our brand to be visible at events, and ultimately these offerings lead to more business for us. But the key reason why we donate is really that we want to support good causes doing good things.

The way I see it, as entrepreneurs, we're obligated to help people. I'm certainly no liberal hippy, but it bothers me when I see extremely successful businesspeople who continue adding to their second McMansion on the beach while they're laying off staff—business owners who make vast sums of money as a result of their team's work and are perfectly happy not financially lifting up that team. It's fascinating to me how free we are, in starting a business, to affect the world around us. Our innovations literally have the power to change the everyday lives of an untold number of fellow human beings, even if we're just talking about the members of your professional team. Every single one of us is in the middle of some kind of a process. Every single person on this planet is in the process of becoming the next version of themselves; our very society is in the process of becoming the next version of itself. It's up to us as industry leaders to help the evolution of this process along in such a way that we ensure this next version is the best possible version.

This responsibility to help others through business, although becoming more popular as a concept, still isn't given nearly enough attention. That's why I'm so passionate about participating in and spreading the word about programs like MARC, a nonprofit organization devoted to providing opportunities and improving quality of life for individuals with mental and physical disabilities. Because MARC's clients are somewhat limited in their work capacity—but still deserve the chance to make their own money and experience a measure of financial independence—they're always looking for new employment opportunities. And because we bottle our moonshine by hand, we have several positions on our production floor involving simple, repetitive tasks that, although perhaps not particularly appealing to the average job-seeker, present just the right amount of a challenge for disabled workers. So Onyx struck up a partnership with MARC in 2013, and the collaboration has been nothing but a win-win for both sides. Not only does the program actually bring our MARC employees here with a supervisor, the state pays a portion of their wages while we pay the rest. That's what I mean by a win-win: We win because we're getting our bottles labeled at a lower price, and our MARC staff wins because they're able to earn some of their own money—and they have a blast doing it! Plus, our regular staff loves having MARC workers around because they're so incredibly upbeat, sweet, and kind. I can't imagine too many other distilleries enjoy regular dancing and hugs on the production line! It's a huge morale boost. Our partnership has brought positive press both to Onyx and MARC; we were featured in a national NPR story because of our unique partnership with MARC, for example. And we win one more time if we educate just one business owner or entrepreneur who didn't know about MARC and inspire them to implement it as well. If everything goes according to plan, our affiliation with MARC will be just the beginning. One of our current insatiable horizons was inspired by our distiller, Kent, who has an autistic daughter. Someday, we hope to open a home for autistic individuals near our distillery, so these individuals can live (with supervision, perhaps from a rotating roster of parents or other family members) and work and make lives for themselves in a permanent, wholesome environment.

Certainly, the financial piece of your business puzzle needs to be in place before you can really think about helping anybody else. After all, philanthropy is defined as "the desire to promote the welfare of others, expressed especially by the generous donation of money to good causes." Without financials—without cold, hard cash—the whole good works machine is paused. That's true on both a business level and a personal level. If you personally don't have financial freedom, you can't emotionally create. Of course, money isn't the most important piece of your happiness pie; it's just as important to factor in the mental and physical freedom you need to be mobile and create. But you have to be driving toward profitability at all times. Make money for your employees, your investors, your brand. Your brand will die without money. Still, there's always room to give. Would it make sense at our stage to write a bunch of big, fat checks to nonprofits? No, but it makes sense for us to donate Onyx to nonprofit events, particularly those that will help to increase our visibility.

When it comes down to it, however, an ongoing commitment to sustainability doesn't need to cost you very much capital at all. It's all a matter of the choices you make, both large and small. For example, our labels are printed down the road from our distillery by a local company, which is one small but significant way we stimulate the local economy. The bottles themselves aren't locally produced, but they are American made—a sustainable choice that wasn't even ours to make for awhile. You may not be aware of this, but there was very little glass being produced in America for quite some time, which meant that when Onyx launched, we were forced to order our bottles from Germany; the other options were Mexico and China, both of which offered a lower-quality product. So even though, as I said, we had little choice in the matter but to import our bottles, the concept thoroughly bugged me. Just think of all the fossil fuels required to load cases and cases of glass bottles on trucks in Germany, drive them to a port, load them on a boat, sail them to New York, unload them again, drive them across state lines—you see where I'm going with this. The process was horribly inefficient, and the inherent wastefulness tugged sharply at my sense of social responsibility. Luckily, I wasn't the only one who felt that way, and before long, an American glass-making company opened up shop to meet the growing demand for bottles born in the United States. Thanks to that company, we're now saving money, burning less fossil fuels, and supporting our nation's economy to boot. Plus, we're giving our customers the satisfaction of buying an American-made product.

Nowadays, with 6 billion people on the planet and a surplus of companies that don't necessarily have a commitment to quality, a little authenticity goes a long way. And low-quality products aren't even the worst of it. I'm truly overwhelmed by how many unethical companies are out there right now selling potentially dangerous products just to make a buck. That, in my mind, is the definition of *un*sustainable entrepreneurship. If you're a successful founder of a company and you, personally, are financially free—as in, you have more money than you could ever really hope to spend—I don't understand being in business for any other reason than wanting to affect change in a positive way. Among my heroes in this regard are Warren Buffett and Bill Gates, who convinced some of the world's wealthiest individuals to join them in a "Giving Pledge" that requires the donation of half of their vast fortunes to charity; other members of this billionaires' club include Michael Bloomberg, Barron Hilton, and George Lucas. These philanthropists are the polar opposite of the miser mentioned in the old Scottish poem we talked about, the one containing my family motto. These generous figures are anything but misers too busy hoarding their "pelf" to enjoy life.

You can get pretty far in life being selfish, but I don't know that you can get to the very top. One thing I always tell young people who think they might have a future in business is "Go wait tables." Learn the value of serving others, and the joy that comes with serving others well. The joy is in the chore. If you have a mindset that you're too good or too important to serve others, well, you're going to lose your way. Onyx isn't a business behemoth on the level of Microsoft (yet!), so I'm not fielding messages from Warren Buffett asking me to donate a portion of my fortune to make the world a better place (yet!), but that doesn't mean Onyx as a company can't do its part. Recently, we started planting corn to use in our moonshine on Pete's family's farm in Wethersfield. The crop won't fill our entire demand, but it will supply a piece of what we need, thereby helping to make our business more self-sustainable. Not only that, our pesticide-free growing practices are both helping the earth and helping our team to grow as strong as those stalks of grain. There's nothing like spending time together in the fields, the hot sun shining on our heads as Pete's dad readies the ground in his 1920s-era red tractor.

Our foray into farming illustrates what I believe to be another part of sustainability, which is helping to define your startup's culture from the start. One of the ways you can do that is through a series of moments and experiences that make your team members feel good and differentiate your product; if you can manage to do something for the world at large in the process, all the better.

Earlier, I mentioned our space project. To commemorate Earth Day 2015, we'll be launching a full-sized bottle of our moonshine into space. An endeavor two years in the making, the launch will involve sending the 750-milliliter bottle (along with a rocks glass!) 22 miles above Earth, mounted on a silver platter. The project took quite a bit of time and effort. We enlisted a team of scientists to construct a custom-built, weather balloon-powered space apparatus called "Onyx 1" that has been fitted with GoPro cameras, GPS, a radar deflector, a deployable parachute, and a protective foam casing that will safeguard the bottle upon its eventual landing in the Long Island Sound; after landing, the bottle will be recovered and displayed at our headquarters. Let's face it: The last thing Long Island Sound needs is one more bottle floating in its already polluted waters—even if that bottle is labeled by hand and made from American glass!

Onyx Moonshine is all about attempting things that haven't been done before, and that, to me, is the true essence of the American Spirit. It's amazing to think that 150 years ago our ancestors were arrested for illegally selling moonshine and here we are, legally sending a bottle into space! The human race has accomplished so much, and this space launch is a tribute to that fact, as well as a reminder that we can continue to accomplish great things through sustainable means.

And thus concludes my 10-chapter rant. I've done my best to share a bit of my crazy journey and some modest tidbits of wisdom I somehow was able to figure out along the way. I had to get these thoughts out of my head and onto paper, and if I was able to inspire just one of you to get out there and kick some butt, I'll consider it a big win. Memento mori: Remember that we are all mortal and the day will come when it's our last. So today is the day for you to get started with your venture, for you to make a difference and create the vibrant life you know deep inside you can. Along the way you will have failures; you'll have huge wins; you'll have adventures and meet some incredibly interesting people. Trust me when I say this: It's worth every single second. Now put the book down, and go make it happen!

. P.S. If you end up getting into the spirits, wine, or beer business, feel free to reach out to me—with a sample, of course.

Cheers!

Adam

Cherry Bomb (Shot)

1 oz. Onyx Moonshine
1 oz. maraschino cherry juice
Dash of Tabasco

Sweet, spicy—what more do you need? This one will go down just a little too easily.

INDEX

Absolute responsibility, 146
AdChem Manufacturing Technologies, 88
Advertising, 71, 185-194
Advice, asking for, 124
Advisory board, 206-208, 211-215
Aesthetics, functionality vs., 61
Agreement, operating, 93, 129
Alexander the Great, 156
Allan S. Goodman, 71, 82-84, 86-76
American Spirit, 15-19, 233
Angel investors, 130, 131
Annie's Organic Macaroni & Cheese, 59
Apple MacBook Air, 65
Apple, 200
Art of distilling, 63-64
Attitude, 19
Authenticity, 175, 179, 181, 184, 185-186, 195, 203
Bacardi, 172
Benefits, features vs., 153
Blake, Prestley, 11-12
Bloomburg, Michael, 231
Board of advisors, 206-208, 211-215
Board of directors, 212
Branson, Richard, 140
Brathwait, 187-189

Brathwait, Richard, 188
Brown-Forman, 172
Budweiser, 179-180
Buffett, Warren, 230, 231
Bureau of Alcohol, Tobacco, Tax, and Trade Bureau, 101
Business partnerships, 91-95
Business plan, 119-121
Buzz, 79-80
Carnegie, Dale, 12
CEOS, entrepreneurs vs., 87-88
Chafee & Company Distillers, 54
Chafee & Company Distilling, 171
Chaffee & Co. c. United States, 54
Chafee, Herbert Fuller, 55
Chafee, Jarius Charles, 55, 117
Churchill, Winston, 144, 151
Cirno, Ray, 211
Coggshll, Deb, 89-90
College, failing out of, 12, 34-37
Commitment, 157
Communication, 93
Connecticut Small Brand Council, 104-105
Connecticut State Department of Economic and Community Development, 134-135

Connection, emotional, 187

Consciousness, social, 221-234

Cortés, Hernán, 156

Craft of Whiskey Distilling, The, 63

Cupcake Wars, 192

Customer demand, 147-148

Cycle of mentorship, 207

Delegation, 29

Dell, Michael, 33

Demand, customer, 147-148

Diageo, 172

Diageo, 81, 84

Directors, board of, 212

Discipline, 17

Disney, Walt, 164-165

Distilling, the art of, 63-64

Distribution, 81-87

Donovan, Mike, 74, 82-84, 86-87

Education, 31-33

Einstein, Albert, 31-32

Elon Musk, 164

Emotional connection, 187

Employees, healthy, 223

Employees, potential, 90-91

E-Muscle, 41-42

Entrepreneurs, CEOs vs., 87-88

Events, promotional, 195-196

Extraction, idea, 167-168

Facebook, 144, 162, 194, 200

Failing out of college, 12, 34-37

Failure, 143-159

Features, benefits vs., 153

Financial freedom, 111, 228

Financial projections, 136-137

Friendly's, 11

Functionality, aesthetics vs., 61

Funding, 58-60

Gates, Bill, 230

Giving Pledge, 230-231

Goals, 106-107, 110

GoFundMe, 133

Grammys, 192-193

Greed, 185

Grey Goose, 73, 152

Growth, 136

Happiness, 111

Hard work, 33

Hardcore Sweet Cupcakes, 192

Healthy employees, 223

Helping others, 225-226

Hilton, Barron, 231

Home, working from, 223-224

How to Win Friends and Influence People, 12, 33

Hublein Company, 62

Idea extraction, 167-168

Idea notebook, 165

Individual customer need, 152-154

Insatiable horizon, 97-115

Instagram, 194

Investors, 117-140

Jack Daniels, 72, 74, 82

Jagged Edge, 43

Jay-Z, 43

Jefferson, Thomas, 12

Jobs, Steve, 140

Kickstarter, 133

Kowalczyk, Pete, 38-39, 41, 42-45, 47-48, 51, 52, 55, 59, 61, 67, 69-70, 80,

82-85, 91-95, 97, 99, 103, 136, 139, 145-146, 149-151, 162, 168-169, 170-175, 176, 191, 206, 211, 215, 231-232
Label design, 66
Lead time, 121-122
Legacy, 57
Limoncello, 67-69, 74, 125, 173-174, 177
Lucas, George, 231
Luck, 166
MacFarlane, Seth, 193-194
Managing people, 30
Mann, Horace, 217
Manufacturing process, 60-62
MARC, 226-227
Media, relationships with the, 185
Mentorship, 207
Mercedes, 65-66
Micromanaging, 139, 205
Mission, 56
Money, 117-140
Moonshine Report, The, 191
Moonshine, Southern vs. New England, 52-54
Motivation, 62
Need, individual customer, 152-154
Networking, 208-210
Notebook for ideas, 165
Notebook, keeping a, 108-109
Onyx Soundlab, 44-48, 58, 66, 171
Operating agreement, 93, 129
Opportunity, 16, 33, 183-200
Organic networking, 209

Others, helping, 225-226
Owens, Bill, 63
Partnerships, 95
People, managing, 30
Pernod Ricard, 172
Philanthropy, 228
Philosophy, 56
Pinterest, 194
Planning sequence, reverse, 148-149
Polo, Michael, 88-89
Pop Evil, 191-192
Positive reinforcement, 217
Potential employees, 90-91
PR, 68
Pres releases, 190, 199
Pricing, 46, 73
Pricing, perceived value and, 46
Profitability, 88
Profits, reinvesting, 30
Prohibition, 53, 117-118, 169-170
Projections, financial, 136-137
Promise, life-changing, 98
Promotional events, 195-196
Pull, 84-86, 187, 200
R&D, 121-122
Reading, 31
Reinventing the wheel, 161-181
Reinvesting profits, 30
Relationships with the media, 185
Reputation, 127
Responsibility, absolute, 146
Reverse planning sequence, 148-149
Risk, 157
Rohn, Jim, 209

Roles, clearly defined, 93
Roosevelt, Teddy, 210
Sale, long-term customer vs.
    a, 200
SBA, the, 120
Scalability, 136
SCORE, 120
Secret Stash Whiskey, 79, 121
Seizing opportunity, 183-200
Selfishness, 231
Shark Tank, 122
Smirnoff, 62, 73, 178
Social consciousness, 221-234
Social media, 145, 194-195, 197
Stephens, Robert, 185
Success, 16, 23, 144, 148, 166,
    216-217, 219
Sun Chips, 59
Sustainability, 228-230
Team, your, 209-210, 223-224

Telecommuting, 223-224
Terms sheet, 129
Tracy, Brian, 165
Twitter, 194
Vacation time, 223
Value, pricing and perceived, 46
Venture capitalists, 128, 132,
    139, 215
Vision, 57, 107, 125
Vodka, 67-68, 69, 74, 125, 172-
    173, 177-178
Wheel, reinventing the,
    161-181
Whiskey, 177-178
Whole Foods, 187
Word of mouth, 194
Working from home, 223-224
Writing a business plan,
    119-121
Yukon Jack, 62
Zeitgeist, 175, 183

ABOUT THE AUTHOR

Failing out of college after one semester, Adam von Gootkin chose to embark on an entrepreneurial adventure that has traversed e-commerce, muscle cars, and the music industry. Now, at 32 years young, he and his business partner have resurrected his family moonshine legacy 78 years after its inception, successfully introducing the world to the first ultra-premium American moonshine.

Adam's roots in the spirits industry run deep: His ancestors were arrested in 1864 for tax evasion on a shipment of moonshine bound for Canada, resulting of the collapse of the family business, Chafee & Company Distilling. Undaunted by their demise, the clan opened the grand Chafee's Hotel in Middletown, Connecticut, at the dawn of the Roaring '20s, that hosted an opulent and infamous speakeasy.

Driven by a commitment to sustainable entrepreneurship and a heartfelt desire to make the world a better place, Adam's vision involves constant innovation and an ongoing effort to revive the American Spirit. Through Onyx, he works with many nonprofits and other organizations that strive to help others reach their potential. His story is proof the American Dream is alive and well, and available to anyone with the courage to follow it. In an effort to take his message to the masses, Adam has appeared on numerous national and regional media outlets, including Bloomberg, Fox, and NBC; hosted a regular radio show on Howard Stern's debut radio station, The Rock 106.9.

Adam is sometimes accompanied by his ghost, Rockwell, the original inhabitant of his historic home in Bristol, Connecticut.